1st Workshop on Automatic Spoken Language Translation in Real-World Settings 2021

Held at MT Summit 2021

Online
16 – 20 August 2021

ISBN: 978-1-7138-3923-1

Printed from e-media with permission by:

Curran Associates, Inc.
57 Morehouse Lane
Red Hook, NY 12571

Some format issues inherent in the e-media version may also appear in this print version.

Printed with permission by Curran Associates, Inc. (2022)

For permission requests, please contact the Association for Computational Linguistics at the address below.

Association for Computational Linguistics
209 N. Eighth Street
Stroudsburg, Pennsylvania 18360

Phone: 1-570-476-8006
Fax: 1-570-476-0860

acl@aclweb.org

Additional copies of this publication are available from:

Curran Associates, Inc.
57 Morehouse Lane
Red Hook, NY 12571 USA
Phone: 845-758-0400
Fax: 845-758-2633
Email: curran@proceedings.com
Web: www.proceedings.com

MT SUMMIT VIRTUAL 2021

Proceedings of Machine Translation Summit XVIII

https://mtsummit2021.amtaweb.org

1st Workshop on Automatic Spoken Language Translation in Real-World Settings

Organizers:
Claudio Fantinuoli and Marco Turchi

1st Automatic Spoken Language Translation in Real-World Settings

Organizers
Claudio Fantinuoli fantinuoli@uni-mainz.de
Mainz University/KUDO Inc.

Marco Turchi turchi@fbk.eu
Fondazione Bruno Kessler

1 Aim of the conference

To date, the production of audio-video content may have exceeded that of written texts. The need to make such content available across language barriers has increased the interest in spoken language translation (SLT), opening up new opportunities for the use of speech translation applications in different settings and for different scopes, such as live translation at international conferences, automatic subtitling for video accessibility, automatic or human-in-the-loop respeaking, or as a support system for human interpreters, to name just a few. Furthermore, specific needs are emerging in terms of user profiles, e.g. people with different abilities, and user experiences, e.g. use on mobile devices.

Against this backdrop, the Spoken Language Translation in Real-World Settings workshop aims to bring together researchers in the areas of computer science, translation, and interpreting, as well as users of SLT applications, such as international organizations, businesses, broadcasters, content media creators, to discuss the latest advances in speech translation technologies from both the perspective of the Computer Science and the Humanities, raising awareness on topics such as the challenges in evaluating current technologies in real-life scenarios, customization tools to improve performance, ethical issues, human-machine interaction, and so forth.

2 Invited Speakers

2.1 Marcello Federico, Amazon AI

Recent Efforts on Automatic Dubbing

Automatic dubbing (AD) is an extension of automatic speech-to-speech translation such that the target artificial speech is carefully aligned in terms of duration, lip movements, timbre, emotion, and prosody of the original speaker in order to achieve audiovisual coherence. Dubbing quality strongly depends on isochrony, i.e., arranging the target speech utterances to exactly match the duration of the original speech utterances. In my talk, I will overview ongoing research on AD at Amazon, while focusing on the following aspects: verbosity of machine translation and prosodic alignment. Controlling the output length of MT is crucial in order to generate utterances of the same duration of the original speech. The goal of prosodic alignment is instead to segment the translation of a source sentence into phrases, so that isochrony is achieved without negatively impacting on the speaking rate of the synthetic speech. Along my talk, I will present experimental results and demo videos on four dubbing directions – English to French, Italian, German and Spanish.

Bio

Marcello Federico is a Principal Applied Scientist at Amazon AI, USA, since 2018. He received the Laurea degree in Information Sciences, summa cum laude, from the University of Milan, Italy, in 1987. At Amazon, he leads a research project on automatic dubbing and oversees the science work behind the Amazon Translate service. His research expertise is in automatic dubbing, machine translation, speech translation, language modeling, information retrieval, and speech recognition. In these areas, he co-authored 225 scientific publications, contributed in 20 international and national projects, mostly as scientific leader, and co-developed open source software packages for machine translation (Moses) and language modeling (IRSTLM) used worldwide by research and industry. He has served on the program committees of all major international conferences in the field of human language technology. Since 2004, he is on the steering committee of the International Conference on Spoken Language Translation (IWSLT) series. He has also been editor-in-chief of the ACM Transactions on Audio, Speech and Language Processing; associate editor for Foundations and Trends in Information Retrieval, and a senior editor for the IEEE/ACM Transactions on Audio, Speech, and Language Processing. He has been a board member of the Cross Lingual Information Forum and the European Association for Machine Translation (chair of EAMT 2012), founding officer of the ACL SIG on Machine Translation. He is currently President of the ACL SIG on Spoken Language Translation and associate editor of the Journal of Artificial Intelligence Research. He is a senior member of the IEEE and of the ACM.

2.2 Prof. Silvia Hansen-Schirra, Mainz University

CompAsS - Computer-Assisted Subtitling

With growing research interest and advances in automatic speech recognition (ASR) and neural machine translation (NMT) and their increasing application particularly in the captioning of massive open online resources, implementing these technologies in the domain of TV subtitling is becoming more and more interesting. The CompAsS project aims at researching and optimizing the overall multilingual subtitling process for offline public TV programmes by developing a multimodal subtitling platform leveraging state-of-the-art ASR, NMT and cutting-edge translation management tools. Driven by scientific interest and professional experience, the outcome will reduce resources required to re-purpose high-quality creative content for new languages, allowing subtitling companies and content producers to be more competitive in the international market. Human and machine input will be combined to make the process of creating interlingual subtitles as efficient and fit for purpose as possible from uploading the original video until burning in the final subtitles. Post-editing of written texts is standard in the translation industry, but is typically not used for subtitles. By post-editing subtitles, the project hopes to make significant gains in productivity while maintaining acceptable quality standards. The planned pipeline foresees the use of ASR as a first step for automatic film transcript extraction, followed by human input, which converts the ASR texts into monolingual subtitles. These subtitles are then translated via NMT into English as relay language and several target languages (e.g., German) and finally post-edited. From a scientific perspective, the CompAsS project evaluates the multimodal text processing of movie transcription with automatic-speech recognition and neural machine translation. Applying well-established methods from translation process research, such as keylogging, eye tracking, and questionnaires, this study provides the basis for the interface design of the CompAsS subtitling tool. We investigate how professional subtitlers and translation students work under eight different conditions: two transcription, three translation and three post-editing tasks. We use established measures based on gaze and typing data (i.e. fixations, pauses, editing time, and subjective ratings) in order to analyze the impact of ASR and NMT on cognitive load, split attention and efficiency.

Bio

Silvia Hansen-Schirra is Professor for English Linguistics and Translation Studies and Director of the Translation Cognition (TraCo) Center at Johannes Gutenberg University Mainz in Germersheim. She is the co-editor of the book series "Translation and Multilingual Natural Language Processing" and "Easy – Plain – Accessible". Her research interests include machine translation, accessible communication and translation process research.

2.3 Juan Pino, Facebook AI

End-to-end Speech Translation at Facebook

End-to-end speech translation, the task of directly modeling translation from audio in one language to text or speech in another language, presents advantages such as lower inference latency but faces a data scarcity challenge, including for high resource languages. In this talk, various data and modeling solutions are presented in order to overcome this challenge. Similar to the textual machine translation case, multilingual speech translation provides maintainability and quality improvements for lower resource language pairs. We present our initial efforts on this topic. As simultaneous speech translation is a prerequisite for practical applications such as simultaneous interpretation, we also give an overview of our investigations into end-to-end simultaneous speech translation. Finally, we describe initial work on speech translation modeling for speech output.

Bio Juan Pino is a Research Scientist at Facebook, currently working on speech translation. He received his PhD in machine translation from the University of Cambridge under the supervision of Prof. Bill Byrne.

2.4 Prof. Bart Defrancq, Ghent University

Will it take another 19 years? Cognitive Ergonomics of Computer-Assisted Interpreting (CAI)

In 1926 the first experiments were held where interpreters were required to interpret diplomatic speeches (semi)- simultaneously. Different experimental setups were put to the test to study interpreters' performances and simultaneous interpreting was successfully carried on from 1928 on in different diplomatic contexts (Baigorri-Jalón 2014). However, the real breakthrough only came in 1945 with the Nüremberg trials, where simultaneous interpreting was offered for weeks in a row and served as a model for the organisation of standing diplomatic conferences. Recent years have seen the development of the first usable CAI-tools for simultaneous interpreters, based on automatic speech recognition (ASR) technologies. These tools provide interpreters not with full transcripts of speeches but rather with lists of specific target items that pose problems, such as numbers, terms and named entities. Full transcripts are of little use for simultaneous interpreters as they are working with extremely narrow time frames with regard to the source text and combine several cognitive, language-related tasks. Adding the (language-related) task of consulting a running transcript of the source speech would probably over-burden cognitive processing in interpreters. Experiments with simulated ASR and ASR prototypes have shown that the provision of targeted information improves interpreters' performances on the accuracy dimension with regard to the rendition of the target items (Desmet et al. 2018, Fantinuoli Defrancq 2021). The first analyses of cognitive load associated with consulting ASR while interpreting suggest that no additional cognitive load is involved with the use of the prototype ASR. However, all aforementioned studies were conducted in quasi-experimental settings, with carefully presented speeches by native and near-native speakers, in physical interpreting booths and using prototypes whose features are based on intuition rather than on ergonomic analysis. There is a real risk that in the absence of systematic ergonomic analysis, CAI-tools will face the same fate as simultaneous interpreting technology. In my contribution I will apply Cañas' (2008) principles of cognitive ergonomics to the integration of ASR in interpreting booths or remote simultaneous interpreting (RSI) platforms. According to Cañas, successful integration of software in the human workflow relies on 4 requirements: it should (1) shorten the time to accomplish interaction tasks; (2) reduce the number of mistakes made by humans; (3) reduce learning time; and (4) improve people's satisfaction with a system. Cognitive ergonomics seeks improvement in those areas to make the execution of the overall task assigned to what is called the "Joint Cognitive System", i.e. the joint processing by humans and devices involved in that task (Woods Hollnagel 2006), more successful. I will argue that although the first research results based on data from physical booths are encouraging, the integration of ASR in the interpreters' workflow on RSI platforms will face particular challenges.

References

Baigorri-Jalón, J. (2014). From Paris to Nuremberg. The Birth of Conference Interpreting. Amsterdam: Benjamins. Cañas, J. (2008). Cognitive Ergonomics in Interface Development Evaluation. Journal of Universal Computer Science, 14 (16): 2630-2649.

Defrancq, B., Fantinuoli, C. (2020). Automatic speech recognition in the booth: Assessment of system performance, interpreters' performances and interactions in the context of numbers. Target 33(1): 73-102.

Desmet, B., Vandierendonck, M., Defrancq, B. (2018). Simultaneous interpretation of numbers and the impact of technological support. In Interpreting and technology (pp. 13–27). Language Science Press.

Woods, D. Hollnager, E. (2006). Joint Cognitive Systems: Patterns in Cognitive Systems Engineering. Boca Raton: CRC Press.

Bio

Born in 1970, studied Romance Philology at Ghent University (1987-1991) and was granted a PhD in Linguistics at the same University in 2002. Worked at the College of Europe as a French lecturer from 1992 until 1995, as a researcher at Ghent University from 1995 until 2007, as a visiting professor at the Université Catholique de Louvain-la-Neuve from 2004 until 2009 and as a postdoctoral researcher at Hogeschool from 2007 until 2010. Trained as a conference interpreter in 2010 and was appointed as an assistant professor of interpreting and translation the same year. Has been head of interpreter training both at the masters' and at the postgraduate levels since 2010, both at Hogeschool Gent and University Ghent (since 2013, when the department was moved from the Hogeschool to the University in the framework of an institutional reform). Is a member of the Department Board, the Faculty Board, the Research Commission of the alpha-Faculties, the Doctoral School Board and of the CIUTI Board.

3 Scientific committee

- Nguyen Bach Alibaba US
- Laurent Besacier University of Grenoble
- Dragos Ciobanu University of Vienna
- Jorge Civera Universitat Politècnica de València
- Marta R. Costa-jussà Universitat Politècnica de Catalunya
- Bart Defrancq Ghent University
- Marco Gaido Fondazione Bruno Kessler
- Hirofumi Inaguma University of Kyoto
- Alfons Juan Universitat Politècnica de València

- Alina Karakanta Fondazione Bruno Kessler
- Evgeny Matusov AppTek
- Jan Niehues University of Maastricht
- Sara Papi Fondazione Bruno Kessler
- Franz Pöchhacker University of Vienna
- Bianca Prandi Johannes Gutenberg-Universität Mainz
- Pablo Romero-Fresco Universidade de Vigo
- Juan Pino Facebook
- Claudio Russello UNINT - Rome
- Matthias Sperber Apple
- Sebastian Stueker Karlsruhe Institute of Technology S
- hinji Watanabe Johns Hopkins University

Contents

Seed Words Based Data Selection for Language Model Adaptation

Roberto Gretter, Marco Matassoni, Daniele Falavigna
Fondazione Bruno Kessler, Trento, Italy
(gretter,matasso,falavi)@fbk.eu

Abstract

We address the problem of language model customization in applications where the ASR component needs to manage domain-specific terminology; although current state-of-the-art speech recognition technology provides excellent results for generic domains, the adaptation to specialized dictionaries or glossaries is still an open issue. In this work we present an approach for automatically selecting sentences, from a text corpus, that match, both semantically and morphologically, a glossary of terms (words or composite words) furnished by the user. The final goal is to rapidly adapt the language model of an hybrid ASR system with a limited amount of in-domain text data in order to successfully cope with the linguistic domain at hand; the vocabulary of the baseline model is expanded and tailored, reducing the resulting OOV rate. Data selection strategies based on shallow morphological seeds and semantic similarity via word2vec are introduced and discussed; the experimental setting consists in a simultaneous interpreting scenario, where ASRs in three languages are designed to recognize the domain-specific terms (i.e. dentistry). Results using different metrics (OOV rate, WER, precision and recall) show the effectiveness of the proposed techniques.

1 Introduction

In this paper we describe an approach to adapt the Language Models (LMs) used in a system designed to give help to simultaneous interpreters. Simultaneous interpreting is a very difficult task that requires a high cognitive effort especially to correctly translate parts of the source language that convey important pieces of information for the final users. These are: numerals, named entities and technical terms specific of each interpretation session. As an example, a study reported in Desmet et al. (2018) claims that the error rate made by professional interpreters on the translation of numbers is, on average, equal to 40%.

This demands for a technology, based on automatic speech recognition (ASR), capable of detecting, in real time and with high accuracy, the important information (words or composite terms) of a speech to interpret and to provide it to a professional interpreter by means of a suitable interface. Therefore, our goal is not to minimise the word error rate (WER) of an audio recording, as usual in ASR applications, instead we aim to maximise the performance of the developed system, in terms of precision, recall and F-measure, over a set of "important" terms to recognise, as will be explained in section 4. To do this we experimented on a set of data properly labelled by human experts.

It is worth to point out that this task is different from the usually known "keywords spotting" task, since we cannot assume to know in advance the terms to spot inside the audio stream but we can only start from some "seed" terms belonging to a glossary which is part of the experience of each human interpreter. This demands for further processing modules that: *a)* extend, in some way, the given glossary including also "semantically" similar terms, as will be explained in section 2.2, in order to adapt both the dictionary and the language model (LM) employed in the ASR system, and/or *b)* detect along an automatically generated transcription the pieces of information (i.e. numerals, named entities, etc) useful to the interpreter. Actually, the ASR system described below is part of a bigger system that integrates natural language processing (NLP) modules, dedicated to both named entity and numeral extraction, and a user interface specifically designed according to the requirements of professional interpreters. This system, named SmarTerp[1], aims to support the simultaneous interpreters in various phases of their activities: the preparation of glossaries, automatic extraction and display of the "important" terms of an interpreting session, post-validation of new entries (Rodríguez et al., 2021).

Related works. As previously mentioned spotting known words from audio recordings is a largely investigated task since the beginning of speech recognition technology (e.g. see works reported in Bridle (1973); Rose and Paul (1990); Weintraub (1995). Basically all these approaches used scores derived from acoustic log-likelihoods of recognised words to take a decision of keyword acceptance or rejection.

More recently, with incoming of neural networks, technologies have begun to take hold based on deep neural networks (Chen et al., 2014), convolutional neural networks (Sainath and Parada, 2015) and recurrent neural networks (Fernandez et al., 2007) to approach keyword spotting tasks. The last frontier is the usage of end-to-end neural architectures capable of modelling sequences of acoustic observations, such as the one described in Yan et al. (2020) or the sequence transformer network described in Berg et al. (2021).

The approach we use for enlarging the dictionary of the ASR system and to adapt the corresponding language model to the application domain is to select and use from a given, possibly very large and general text corpus, the sentences that exhibit a certain "similarity" with the terms included in the glossaries furnished by the interpreters. Similarly to the keyword spotting task, "term based similarity" represents a well investigated topic in the scientific community since many years. A survey of approaches can be found in the work reported in Vijaymeena and Kavitha (2016). Also for this task the advent of neural network based models has allowed significant improvements both in the word representation, e.g. with the approaches described in Mikolov et al. (2013), and in text similarity measures, e.g. as reported in Le and Mikolov (2014); Amin et al. (2019).

Worth to notice is that in the ASR system used for this work we do not search for new texts to adapt the LM, instead, as explained in section 2, we select the adaptation texts from the same corpus used to train the baseline LM. Note also that our final goal is not that to extract the named entities from the ASR transcripts - this task is accomplished by the NLP modules mentioned above - instead it consists in providing to the ASR system a LM more suitable to help the human interpreter of a given event. Also for ASR system adaptation there is an enormous scientific literature, both related to language models and to acoustic models adaptation; here we only refer some recent papers: Song et al. (2019) for LM adaptation and Bell et al. (2021) for a review of acoustic model adaptation approaches, especially related to neural models.

2 Automatic selection of texts

Usually a Language Model (LM) is trained over huge amounts of text data in a given language, e.g. Italian. During the training phase, a fixed lexicon is selected - typically the N most frequent words in the text - and millions or billions of n-grams are stored to give some probability to any possible word sequence. This process allows to build a somehow generic LM, capable to represent the language observed in the text.

[1]The SmarTerp Project is funded by EIT DIGITAL under contract n. 21184

However, interpreters often need to specialise their knowledge on a very specific topic, e.g. dentistry. In this case, they also have to quickly become experts in that particular field. We could say that they need to adapt their general knowledge to that field: this means that, before the event, they have to collect material about that topic, study it, prepare and memorise a glossary of very specific technical terms together with their translations.

The same process holds for an ASR system: it can perform in a satisfactory way in a general situation, but it may fail when encountering technical terms in a specific field. So, it has to be adapted, both in terms of lexicon (it may be necessary to add new terms to the known lexicon) and in terms of word statistics for the new terms.

In the SmarTerp project we are going to explore different adaptation procedures and describe in this paper our preliminary work in this direction. At present, we hypothesise that an interpreter could provide some text and the ASR system will be able to adapt to the corresponding topic in a short time (some hours on a medium computer). This short text could range from a few words to a quite large set of documents that identify that particular topic, depending on the expertise and the attitude of the interpreter. Here are some possibilities:

- just a few technical words;
- a glossary of terms, maybe found with a quick internet search;
- a glossary of technical terms with translations, maybe built over the years by an expert interpreter;
- a set of technical documents, in the desired language.

In a very near future, in SmarTerp a pool of interpreters will be engaged in simulations where they have to provide data that, in a complete automatic way (i.e. without the intervention of some language engineer), will adapt the ASR system for a particular topic. In this work we are testing some tools and procedures in order to provide them some possible solutions, assuming that at least some small text (i.e. a glossary, or even a few words) will be available. From this small text we will derive some *seed words* that will be used, in turn, both to update the dictionary of the ASR system and to select LM adaptation texts from the available training corpora (see Table 2). In detail, we implemented the following procedures (although some of them were not used in the experiments described in this paper):

- selection of **seed words**, i.e. technical words that characterise the topic to be addressed; they are simply the words, in the short text provided by the interpreter, that are not in the initial lexicon, composed of the most frequent N words of that language (128 Kwords, in this paper).
- optional enlargement of the set of **seed words**, either by exploiting shallow morphological information or using neural network approaches like word2vec (Mikolov et al., 2013).
- selection of **adaptation text**, i.e. text sentences in the text corpus that contain at least one of the seed words. Note that we hypothesise not to have new texts belonging to the topic to be addressed, that could be directly used for LM adaptation.
- compilation of an **adapted lexicon** and of an **adapted LM**, obtained exploiting the adaptation text.

2.1 Shallow morphological seed words enlargement

Each initial seed word is replaced by a regular pattern which removes the ending part, to find similar words in the complete dictionary of the corpus. Possible parameters are: N_M, maximum number of similar words retained for each seed; L_M, minimal length of a seed pattern to be considered valid (too short patterns are useless or even dangerous).

Language	CV (h:m)	EuroNews (h:m)	Total Speakers	Running words
English	781:47	68:56	35k	5,742k
Italian	148:40	74:22	9k	1,727k
Spanish	322:00	73:40	16k	2,857k

Table 1: Audio corpora for AM training

2.2 Semantic similarity based approach

Each initial seed word is fed to a pretrained neural skipgram model (word2vect, see http://vectors.nlpl.eu/repository), which returns an embedded representation of words. Then, the N more similar words are computed using the cosine distance between couples of words embeddings. The process can be iterated by feeding word2vec with every new similar word obtained. Possible parameters are: N_W, number of retained words from each term; I_W, number of iterations: typically 1, or 2 in case of a very short list of initial seeds.

2.3 Selection of adaptation text

Given a final set of seed words, the huge text corpus is filtered and every document containing at least one seed word, not contained in the (128K) initial lexicon, is retained. One parameter of the filter - not used in this work - is the number of words forming the context around every seed word in a document. This may be useful to avoid to include in the adaptation corpus useless pieces of texts, due to the fact that every line in the training corpora (newspaper or Wikipedia, title or article) is considered a document, containing from few words to tens (even hundreds in few cases) of Kwords. Note that the selection of the adaptation text is largely responsible of the lexicon enlargement (up to 250 Kwords, see Table 6), since the number of seed words resulted to be, in our preliminary experiments, always below 4 Kwords.

3 ASR systems

The ASR system is based on the popular Kaldi toolkit (Povey et al., 2011), that provides optimised modules for hybrid architectures; the modules support arbitrary phonetic-context units, common feature transformation, Gaussian mixture and neural acoustic models, n-gram language models and on-line decoding.

3.1 Acoustic models

The acoustic models are trained on data coming from CommonVoice (Ardila et al., 2020) and Euronews transcriptions (Gretter, 2014), using a standard *chain* recipe based on lattice-free maximum mutual information (LF-MMI) optimisation criterion (Povey et al., 2016). In order to be more robust against possible variations in the speaking rate of the speakers, the usual *data augmentation* technique for the models has been expanded, generating time-stretched versions of the original training set (with factors 0.8 and 1.2, besides the standard factors 0.9 and 1.1).

Table 1 summarises the characteristics of the audio data used for the models in the three working languages considered in the project.

3.2 Language models and Lexica

Text corpora that can be used to train LMs for the various languages are described in Table 2 and derive both from Internet news, collected from about 2000 to 2020, and from a Wikipedia dump; their corresponding total lexica amount to several millions of words (from 4 to 10) for every language. It has to be clarified that, being the original texts definitely not clean, most of

Language	Lexicon size	Total running words	Internet News	Wikipedia 2018
English	9.512.829	3790.55 Mw	1409.91 Mw	2380.64 Mw
Italian	4.943.488	3083.54 Mw	2458.08 Mw	625.46 Mw
Spanish	4.182.225	2246.07 Mw	1544.51 Mw	701.56 Mw

Table 2: Text corpora for training the LMs for ASR in the three SmarTerp languages. Mw means millions of running words.

the low frequency words are in fact non-words (typos, etc.). For practical reasons, the size of the lexicon used in the ASR usually ranges from 100 to 500 Kwords.

The baseline language models are trained using the huge corpora described in Table 2; the adaptation set is selected from the same huge corpora. After the selection stage, the resulting trigrams are computed and a mixed LM is built and then pruned to reach a manageable size. The adapted LM probabilities are efficiently derived using the approach described in Bertoldi et al. (2001) by interpolating the frequencies of trigrams of the background (i.e. non adapted) LM with the corresponding frequencies computed on the adaptation text.

The most frequent 128Kwords of the corpus are retained; all the words of the adaptation set are then included in the corresponding lexicon.

4 Description of SmarTerp multilingual benchmark

As mentioned above, in SmarTerp we prepared benchmarks for the 3 languages of the project: English, Italian, Spanish. For each language, a number of internet videos having Creative Commons licence were selected, in order to reach at least 3 hours of material on a particular topic, dentistry. Table 3 reports duration and number of words of the benchmarks. Data were collected, automatically transcribed and manually corrected[2] using Transcriber[3], a tool for segmenting, labelling and transcribing speech. In addition to time markers and orthographic transcription of the audio data, we decided to label with parenthesis Important Words (IWs), which represent content words that are significant for the selected domain (i.e. dentistry) and are a fundamental part of the desired output of the automatic system. As only one annotator labelled IWs, it was not possible to compute annotators' agreement for this task. We will address this issue in future works.

language	recordings	raw duration	transcribed duration	running words	running IWs
English	5	04:02:34	03:03:06	28279	3343
Italian	33	05:29:34	04:10:31	31001	4560
Spanish	13	03:09:53	03:01:59	25339	3351

Table 3: Benchmarks collected and annotated in SmarTerp.

Figure 1 shows a screenshot of Transcriber, where some IWs are highlighted: (dentistry), (dental caries), (periodontal diseases), (oral cancer). In the benchmarks, phrases composed up to 6 words were identified as IWs.

[2]We are really grateful to Susana Rodríguez, who did the manual check for all the languages.

[3]http://trans.sourceforge.net/

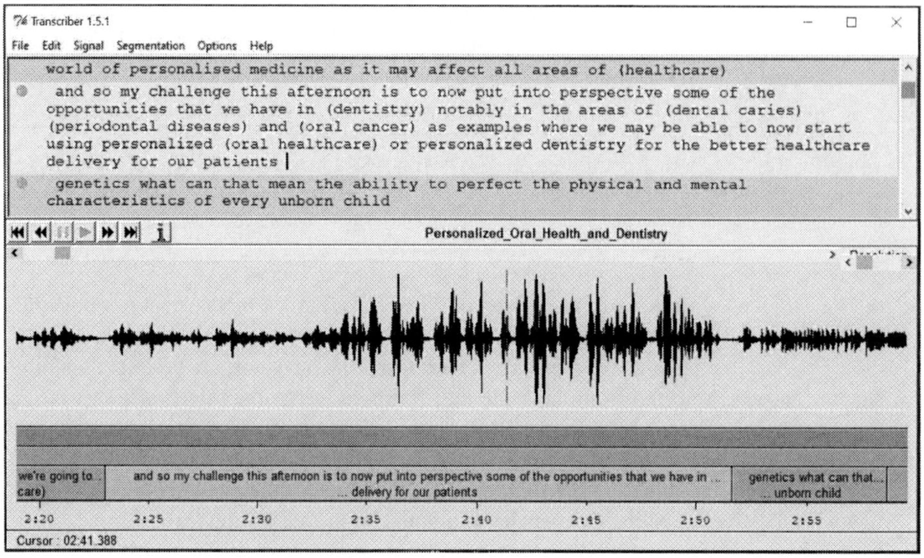

Figure 1: Screenshot of Transcriber, a tool used to manually transcribe the SmarTerp benchmark. In the highlighted segment, IWs are in parentheses.

4.1 IW normalization

In order to be able to consistently evaluate the performance of the system in terms of IWs, and considering that it was impossible to pre-define a fixed set of IW patterns, we decided to implement a procedure that automatically processed the whole benchmark. It consisted of the following basic steps, applied independently for every language:

1. identification of all manually defined IWs in the benchmark;
2. reduction to a minimum set of IWs, by removing ambiguities. Given that A, B, C, etc. are single words, some cases are:
   - if exist (A), (B) and (A B), then the IW (A B) is removed - will be replaced by (A) (B);
   - if exist (C), (D E) and (C D E), then the IW (C D E) is removed;
   - note however that if exist (C), (D E) and (D C E), nothing can be removed.
3. regeneration of the benchmark, by applying the following steps:
   (a) remove all round brackets;
   (b) considering the minimum set of IWs, apply new brackets at every IW occurrence, starting from the longest IWs and ending with the one-word IWs;
   (c) in order to evaluate Precision, Recall and F-measure of IWs, remove all words not inside brackets.

Note that some IWs originally present in the benchmark, although legitimate, could not appear in the final version of the benchmark: suppose that the only occurrence of (B) alone is in the context A (B) and also the IW (A B) exist: after the regeneration of the benchmark, both cases will result (A B).

After the application of this algorithm, a consistent version of the benchmark was obtained. By applying the same regeneration steps to the ASR output, a fair comparison was

REF	the most of **them** referred from (pulmonary specialist) **(ENTs)** (paediatricians) **let's let Boyd try** nothing **else**
ASR	**in** the most of **my** referred from (pulmonary specialist) **ian** (paediatricians) **was led by tried** nothing
ALIGNMENT	I_in S_them_my S_ENTs_ian S_let's_was S_let_led S_Boyd_by S_try_tried D_else (Sub= 6 Ins= 1 Del= 1 REF=16)
WER	50.00% [100 * (6 +1 +1) / 16]
IW-REF	(pulmonary_specialist) **(ENTs)** (paediatricians)
IW-ASR	(pulmonary_specialist) (paediatricians)
P / R / F	Precision 1.00 [2 / 2] / Recall 0.67 [2 / 3] / F-Measure 0.80
Isol-IW-REF	(pulmonary) (specialist) **(ENTs)** (paediatricians)
Isol-IW-ASR	(pulmonary) (specialist) (paediatricians)
P / R / F	Precision 1.00 [3 / 3] / Recall 0.75 [3 / 4] / F-Measure 0.86

Table 4: Evaluation metrics on a sample of the English benchmark: WER over the whole text; Precision, Recall, F-measure over both the IWs and the Isolated-IWs. ASR errors are highlighted in bold. IWs are those in parentheses.

possible, considering only the IWs. We could also consider different metrics, either by considering each IW as a single item (despite the number of words that compose it) or by considering separately each work that compose the IWs (henceforth Isol-IW). Standard evaluation of ASR output is Word Error Rate (WER), resulting from a word-by-word alignment between reference text (REF) and ASR output (TEST). In detail, WER is the percentage of substitution, insertions and deletions over the number of REF words. In SmarTerp, however, it could be more useful to concentrate on the IWs only, and to consider Precision, Recall and F-Measure as primary metric. The example in Table 4 shows the different metrics used in this work.

4.2 Preliminary analysis

Figure 2 reports OOV rate of the SmarTerp Benchmark for different values of the lexicon size, computed on all the available text data described in Table 2. An inspection of OOV words was

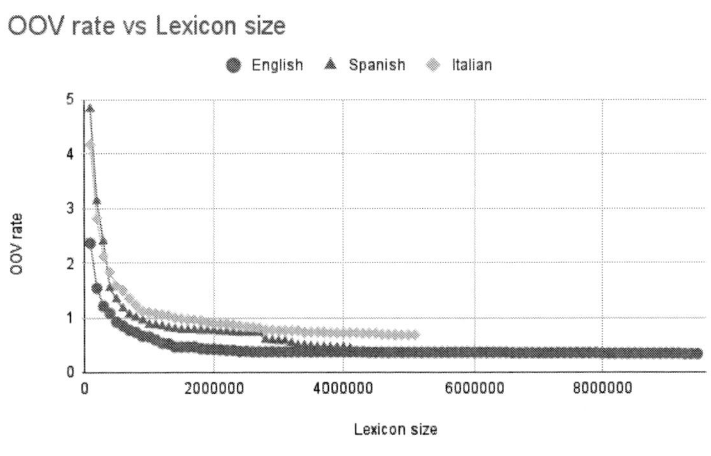

Figure 2: OOV rate of the SmarTerp benchmarks against lexicon size for the 3 languages.

allunghiamo *we lengthen*		distinguerle *distinguish them*		divideremo *we will divide*	
10355	allunga	12118	distingue	7273	divide
12657	allungare	12493	distinguere	7931	dividendo
17187	allungato	20484	distinguono	12286	dividere
18040	allungo	26323	distinguo	14127	dividendi
20126	allungamento	34366	distinguersi	15601	dividono
23870	allungano	52496	distinguendosi	27370	dividersi
25749	allungata	56673	distingueva	43165	divideva
35514	allungando	60858	distinguerlo	59956	dividerà
40996	allungate	61213	distinguendo	61370	dividerci
42540	allungati	67741	distinguibili	62319	divideranno
43104	allungarsi	75608	distinguerla	63369	dividendosi
60394	allunghi	77105	distinguibile	68113	dividevano
98044	allungherà	79891	distinguevano	80977	dividerli
106019	allungava	91152	distinguerli	84294	dividend
120007	allungandosi	115236	distinguiamo	91609	divida
126079	allungherebbe	116550	distingua	97706	dividiamo
		119097	distinguerà	121708	dividerlo

Table 5: Morphological variations of OOV words, known in the 128 Kwords lexicon, along with their position in the lexicon.

done for the Italian language, in order to better understand how the OOV words are distributed among different classes. With respect to the 128 Kwords lexicon, we had that the Italian benchmark is composed of 31001 running words, of which 1089 are OOV (corresponding to 3.51% OOV rate). The number of different OOV words was 474, manually classified as follows:

- **190 Morpho**: morphological variations of common words (e.g. allunghiamo, distinguerle, divideremo - *we lengthen, distinguish them, we will divide*);
- **181 Tech**: technical terms, that will be part of IWs so it is extremely important to keep their number as low as possible (e.g. bruxismo, implantologia, parodontopatici - *bruxism, implantology, periodontal disease*);
- **34 Errors**: words that should not be here and will be fixed soon: numbers in letters, wrong tokenization (e.g. cinque, computer-assistita, impianto-protesica, l'igiene - *five, computer-assisted, implant-prosthetic, the hygiene*);
- **28 English**: terms in English, often they are technical terms and should be recognized (e.g. osteotomy, picking, restaurative, tracing);
- **20 Names**: proper names of people, firms or products (e.g. claronav, davinci, hounsfield, navident);
- **10 Latin**: latin words (e.g. dolor, restitutio, tumor - *pain, restoration, swelling*);
- **8 Acronyms**: (e.g. t-test, mua, d3, d4);
- **3 Foreign**: pseudo-foreign words that need particular care for pronunciation (e.g. customizzata, customizzati, matchare - *Italian neologisms from English custom, match*).

Tech, English, Names, Latin and Foreign will deserve a particular attention in future studies, because they are important for the domain. Errors will be fixed and should disappear; Acronyms should be recognized as subwords (e.g., d3 as d 3). Morpho will probably be misrecognized as another morphological variation of the same stem, present in the active dictionary, which in this domain is not considered a critical error. Note that a single verbal stem in Italian can generate up to 300 different words in Italian, including clitics. In Table 5 you can see the morphological variations of the 3 terms of the class Morpho reported above which are present in the 128 Kwords lexicon.

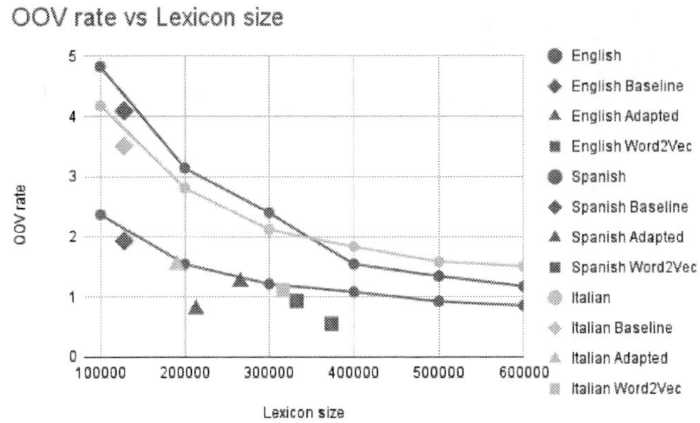

Figure 3: OOV rate of the SmarTerp benchmarks against lexicon size for the 3 languages, for all the experiments and languages.

5 Experiments and results

Since several approaches can be employed to obtain, enlarge and use the seed words (e.g. based on texts distance, texts semantic similarity, etc) we consider the following indicators that allow to measure their effectiveness on the benchmarks collected and manually transcribed within the SmarTerp project.

- Seeds: number of seed words, used to extract the adaptation text:
- Out Of Vocabulary rate (OOV rate): it is the percentage of unknown words in the benchmark, with respect to the lexicon. OOV words cannot be part of the output of the ASR, hence they will be certainly errors. We should try to get a low OOV rate without the lexicon size growing too much;
- Lexicon size: total number of active words in the adapted LM;
- Word Error Rate (WER): it measures the percentage of errors made by the ASR;
- Precision, Recall, F-Measure over the set of Important Words (IWs) that were defined.

The following experiments were carried out for each of the three languages:

- **Baseline**: the initial 128Kwords lexicon and the LM trained on the whole corpus, without any adaptation;
- **Adapted**: LM adapted starting from seed words coming from a dental glossary (normally 2-3 pages of text, resulting into some hundreds of seeds), found with a quick search in internet for terms like "dental glossary" (e.g. https://bnblab.com/intro/terminology).
- **Word2Vec**: LM adapted using seed words obtained from 5 initial seed words, applying two iterations ($I_w = 2$) of the procedure based on semantic similarity and retaining, for each term, $N_w = 40$ words, obtaining $\sim$ 3000 seed words. The 5 magic words[4] were:
  - **English**: tartar, filling, caries, tooth, dentist

[4]Many thanks to Susana Rodríguez for the translations of the magic words from Italian

- **Italian**: tartaro, otturazione, carie, dente, dentista
- **Spanish**: sarro, relleno, caries, diente, dentista

Figure 3 reports OOV rate of the SmarTerp benchmark for different values of the lexicon size for each experiment, along with the initial part of the curve of Figure 2. It should be noted that, for every language, Baseline is along the initial curve, while both Adapted and Word2Vec are well below it. For all languages, Adapted has a Lexicon size which is in between Baseline and Word2Vec. This is due to an initial choice of the parameters described in Section 2: by changing the parameters, a cloud of values could be generated instead of a single point. In fact, in this work we report only initial experiments and future efforts will be devoted to a parameter optimization. In any case, the Lexicon size is directly related to the number of seeds and on the size of the adaptation text, which plays a very important role in the adaptation stage.

Table 6 reports preliminary results on the three benchmarks, for all the experiments. Together with the number of obtained seed words, OOV rate and Lexicon size, we report WER computed on all the uttered words (including functional words, which are useless for this task), and Precision/Recall/F-measure computed both on IWs and Isol-IWs: since they represent the most technically significant words in the domain, they are more related to the output desired by interpreters. It is worth noting that, with respect to Baseline, both the Adapted and Word2Vec systems are effective for all of the three languages and for all the considered metrics. Word2Vec performs slightly better than Adapted, but this can be due to the initial value of the parameters that bring to more seeds and to a bigger Lexicon size. Low WER for English is partly due to a scarce audio quality in the recordings, that mainly affects functional words: this explains the English high precision, which is computed on IWs only.

	Seeds	Lex size	OOVrate	WER	IW P / R / F	Isol-IW P / R / F
Eng BL	0	128041	1.93%	26.39%	0.90 / 0.61 / 0.73	0.96 / 0.59 / 0.73
Eng ada	257	213237	0.79%	23.34%	0.92 / 0.73 / 0.81	0.97 / 0.71 / 0.82
Eng w2v	2999	373956	0.55%	23.86%	0.93 / 0.72 / 0.81	0.97 / 0.70 / 0.81
Ita BL	0	128009	3.51%	15.14%	0.88 / 0.67 / 0.76	0.95 / 0.67 / 0.79
Ita ada	213	190126	1.53%	11.73%	0.96 / 0.84 / 0.89	0.98 / 0.82 / 0.90
Ita w2v	3527	316679	1.11%	11.28%	0.96 / 0.85 / 0.90	0.99 / 0.84 / 0.91
Spa BL	0	128229	4.09%	22.60%	0.86 / 0.56 / 0.68	0.93 / 0.56 / 0.69
Spa ada	673	265764	1.25%	17.74%	0.95 / 0.76 / 0.85	0.98 / 0.75 / 0.85
Spa w2v	3207	333072	0.93%	17.31%	0.95 / 0.79 / 0.86	0.98 / 0.78 / 0.87

Table 6: Preliminary results for Baseline (BL), Adapted (ada) and Word2Vec (w2v) systems. Both WER on all words and Precision/Recall/F-measure on composite and isolated IWs are reported.

6 Conclusions

We described two different approaches for extending the dictionary of an ASR system in order to detect important terms from technical speeches, namely dental reports, to be translated by simultaneous professional interpreters. The two approaches consist in extracting adaptation text from a huge set of text data, starting from some seed words. In the first one, seed words come from a given glossary. The second one is based on the application of a text similarity measure to an initial (very small) set of 5 seed words. After the application of the selection procedures we adapted the language models used in the ASR system employed in a computer assisted interpretation (CAI) system under development and we proved the effectiveness on the approaches in terms of different evaluation metrics.

References

Amin, K., Lancaster, G., Kapetanakis, S., Althoff, K., Dengel, A., and Petridis, M. (2019). Advanced similarity measures using word embeddings and siamese networks in cbr. In *Proc. of IntelliSys*, volume 1038.

Ardila, R., Branson, M., Davis, K., Kohler, M., Meyer, J., Henretty, M., Morais, R., Saunders, L., Tyers, F., and Weber, G. (2020). Common voice: A massively-multilingual speech corpus. In *Proceedings of the 12th Language Resources and Evaluation Conference*, pages 4218–4222, Marseille, France. European Language Resources Association.

Bell, P., Fainberg, J., Klejch, O., Li, J., Renals, S., and Swietojanski, P. (2021). Adaptation algorithms for neural network-based speech recognition: An overview. *IEEE Open Journal of Signal Processing*, 2:33–66.

Berg, A., O'Connor, M., and Cruz, M. T. (2021). Keyword transformer: A self-attention model for keyword spotting.

Bertoldi, N., Brugnara, F., Cettolo, M., Federico, M., and Giuliani, D. (2001). From broadcast news to spontaneous dialogue transcription: Portability issues. In *Proc. of ICASSP*, Salt Lake City, UT(US).

Bridle, J. (1973). An efficient elastic-template method for detecting given words in running speech. In *British acoustical society spring meeting*, pages 1—-4.

Chen, G., Parada, C., and Heigold, G. (2014). Small-footprint keyword spotting using deep neural networks. In *Proc. of ICASSP*, page 4087–4091.

Desmet, B., Vandierendonck, M., and Defrancq, B. (2018). Simultaneous interpretation of numbers and the impact of technological support. In *Interpreting and technology*, pages 13—27, C. Fantinuoli ed. Berlin: Language Science Press.

Fernandez, S., Graves, A., and Schmidhuber, J. (2007). An application of recurrent neural networks to discriminative keyword spotting. In *Artificial Neural Networks – ICANN 2007*, page 220–229.

Gretter, R. (2014). Euronews: a multilingual speech corpus for ASR. In *Proceedings of the Ninth International Conference on Language Resources and Evaluation (LREC'14)*, pages 2635–2638, Reykjavik, Iceland. European Language Resources Association (ELRA).

Le, Q. and Mikolov, T. (2014). Distributed representations of sentences and documents. In *Proc. of International Conference on Machine Learning*, Beijing, China.

Mikolov, T., Chen, K., Corrado, G. S., and Dean, J. (2013). Efficient estimation of word representations in vector space. In *Proc. of NIPS*, volume 2.

Povey, D., Ghoshal, A., Boulianne, G., Burget, L., Glembek, O., Goel, N., Hannemann, M., Motlicek, P., Qian, Y., Schwarz, P., Silovsky, J., Stemmer, G., and Vesely, K. (2011). The kaldi speech recognition toolkit. IEEE Catalog No.: CFP11SRW-USB.

Povey, D., Peddinti, V., Galvez, D., Ghahremani, P., Manohar, V., Na, X., Wang, Y., and Khudanpur, S. (2016). Purely sequence-trained neural networks for ASR based on lattice-free MMI. In *Proc. of INTERSPEECH*, pages 2751–2755.

Rodríguez, S., Gretter, R., Matassoni, M., Falavigna, D., Alonso, Á., Corcho, O., and Rico, M. (2021). SmarTerp: A CAI system to support simultaneous interpreters in real-time. In *Proc. of TRITON 2021*.

Rose, R. and Paul, D. (1990). A hidden markov model based keyword recognition system. In *Proc. of ICASSP*, page 129–132.

Sainath, T. and Parada, C. (2015). Convolutional neural networks for small-footprint keyword spotting. In *Proc. of Interspeech.*

Song, Y., Jiang, D., Zhao, W., Xu, Q., Wong, R. C.-W., and Yang, Q. (2019). Chameleon: A language model adaptation toolkit for automatic speech recognition of conversational speech. In *Proceedings of the 2019 Conference on Empirical Methods in Natural Language Processing and the 9th International Joint Conference on Natural Language Processing (EMNLP-IJCNLP): System Demonstrations*, pages 37–42, Hong Kong, China. Association for Computational Linguistics.

Vijaymeena, M. and Kavitha, K. (2016). A survey on similarity measures in text mining. *Machine Learning and Applications: An International Journal*, 3(1).

Weintraub, M. (1995). Lvscr log-likelihood ratio scoring for keyword spotting. In *Proc. of ICASSP*, volume 1, page 297–300.

Yan, H., He, Q., and Xie, W. (2020). Crnn-ctc based mandarin keywords spotting. In *Proc. of ICASSP 2020*, pages 7489–93.

Post-Editing Job Profiles for Subtitlers

Anke Tardel antardel@uni-mainz.de
Silvia Hansen-Schirra hansenss@uni-mainz.de
Faculty for Translation Studies, Linguistics, and Cultural Studies, Johannes Gutenberg University of Mainz, Germersheim, 76726, Germany
Jean Nitzke jeann@uia.no
Department for Foreign Languages and Translation, University of Agder, Kristiansand, 4630, Norway

Abstract

Language technologies, such as machine translation (MT), but also the application of artificial intelligence in general and an abundance of CAT tools and platforms have an increasing influence on the translation market. Human interaction with these technologies becomes ever more important as they impact translators' workflows, work environments, and job profiles. Moreover, it has implications for translator training. One of the tasks that emerged with language technologies is post-editing (PE) where a human translator corrects raw machine translated output according to given guidelines and quality criteria (O'Brien, 2011: 197-198). Already widely used in several traditional translation settings, its use has come into focus in more creative processes such as literary translation and audiovisual translation (AVT) as well. With the integration of MT systems, the translation process should become more efficient. Both economic and cognitive processes are impacted and with it the necessary competences of all stakeholders involved change. In this paper, we want to describe the different potential job profiles and respective competences needed when post-editing subtitles.

1. Existing translation competence models

In the last decades, different translation competence models have been developed (e.g., PACTE, 2003; Göpferich, 2009; EMT, 2009), which have many competences in common, but also presented some differences (see Table 1). Often, professional translators are not only asked to translate, but also to revise translated texts. Further, MT output has become an established resource in the translation process. Accordingly, expanded competence models have been developed for revision (Robert et al., 2017) and PE (Nitzke et al., 2019) processes.

	PACTE 2003	Göpferich 2009	EMT 2009	Robert et al. 2017	Nitzke et al. 2019
overlapping competences and characteristics	linguistic	language	communicative	bilingual	bilingual
	translation	translation routine activation		translation routine activation	translation
	extra-linguistic	domain	thematic	extralinguistic	extralinguistic
	strategic	strategic		strategic	strategic
	instrumental	tools and research	technological	tools & research	instrumental
			info mining		research
	psycho-physiological	psycho-motor		psycho-physiological	

		translation norms		translation and revision norms	
		translation assignment		translation and revision brief	
		translator self-concept / professional ethos		translator and reviser self-concept / professional ethos	
			translation service provision		service
				revision routine activation	revision
model specific		psycho-physical disposition; motivation		interpersonal; knowledge about translation; knowledge about revision	risk-assessment; consulting; machine translation; post-editing

Table 1: Competences and characteristics according to the different models showing the common competences ("overlapping") and competences that only occur in one of the models (model specific)

As PE is a rather new task in the professional translation market, Nitzke et al.'s (2019) model was rather seen as a starting point for discussing the new field and few adjustments needed to be done. Figure 1 presents the revised model (Nitzke and Hansen-Schirra, in press).

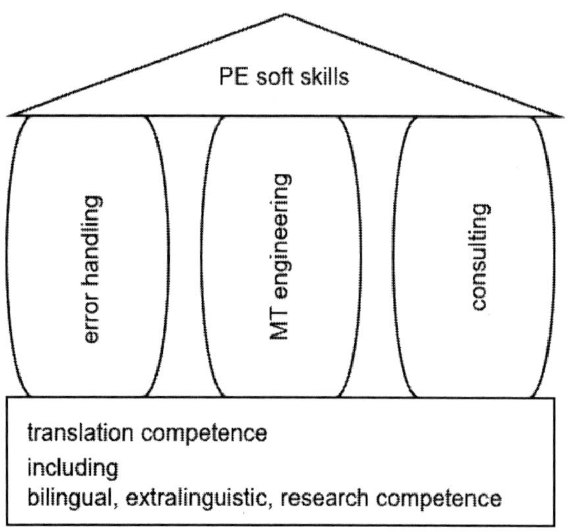

Figure 1: Revised PE model (Nitzke and Hansen-Schirra in press)

The PE model is grounded on the *translation competences*, including bilingual, extralinguistic and research competence. These competences are the foundation of the model, as this is the basis for skilled post-editing. On the foundation stand three columns, which define additional competences. First, *error handling* describes the post-editor's competence to deal with errors in the MT output including error spotting, error classification, but also which errors to correct and how to correct these specific errors. Further, *MT engineering* competence describes not only the knowledge a post-editor needs to have about MT systems but also the ability to train and assess MT systems. Finally, post-editors should be able to *consult* direct clients, companies as well as agencies regarding risk assessment and service competences within the PE task. The model is topped by a figurative roof, the *PE soft skills*. These include, e.g., psycho-physiological components (concentration, attention despite repeated errors, stress, analytical thinking), an affinity towards the latest technological developments, the ability to handle PE briefs including guidelines for the PE task (information on target audience, text type skopos, and required effort), or the post-editor's self-perception and professional work ethos. Depending on the specialisation, these competences may play a major or a minor role resulting in three possible job perspectives, i.e., post-editor, MT engineer, and MT consultant (see Nitzke and Hansen-Schirra in press for more details). Since automation developments also affect AVT processes, the following section applies and further develops the competences needed for post-editing subtitles.

2. Additional competences for post-editing subtitles

Subtitling as a special form of translation is part of the subfield AVT, indicating that the text goes beyond written words and includes both verbal and non-verbal elements in the two audio and visual channels. According to Gottlieb (2005: 36), subtitling is a diasemiotic form of translation of a polysemiotic text. Subtitling may describe intralingual or interlingual translation in that depending on the target audience different elements need to be translated from speech to written text within temporal and spatial constraints within a language or from a source language into a target language. Leaning on the definition by Díaz-Cintas (2020: 150), subtitling, or timed text, can be defined as the added, written, and condensed rendition of aural utterances (and sounds) and on-screen texts in the source or target language in one- to two-line captions displayed usually on the bottom of the screen in synch with the audio and image. This is done according to a particular style guide or guidelines (dictated by national regulations, companies, providers, etc.) which among others prescribe display times and segmentation rules. Further, subtitles may be either verbatim or reduced and prepared ahead of time or live.

In this article, we discuss PE for prepared interlingual subtitling while also referencing to intralingual subtitling and live-(sub)titling as some of the competences overlap.

Subtitling, either way, is a rather complex translation task dealing with polysemiotic text translated from the audiovisual to visual channel and thus requires, in addition to translation competences, specific subtitling competences. While some of the subtitling competences overlap with written translation competences, they can be broken down to the following sub competences according to Merchán's (2018: 471) taxonomy which is based on PACTE's translation competence model:

(1) *contrastive* competences, i.e., an exhaustive knowledge and mastery of the source and target language both in written and oral comprehension including colloquial varieties and dialects;
(2) *extralinguistic* competences, i.e., good knowledge of the cultures involved in the translation process and the target audience; film and theatre knowledge; familiarity with the language of film and visual semiotics as well as various features of different audiovisual texts and genres;

(3) *methodological* and *strategic* competences, i.e., the theoretical knowledge of one or several AVT modes. Here, subtitling includes the mastery of techniques to visualize text and image simultaneously, the capacity of synthesis, i.e., techniques to streamline texts, capacity to use creative language resources and to analyse various genres and reproduce their discursive features (e.g., false orality) and finally mastery of synchronization and spotting techniques for subtitling;
(4) *instrumental* competences, i.e., the mastery of AVT software for subtitling, specific software to digitize, codify and convert audiovisual files, speech recognition (SR) software (speaker-dependent and automatic) and mastery of strategies to retrieve information and other resources;
(5) *translation problem-solving* competences, including knowledge of translation strategies and techniques to translate different audiovisual genres as well as the capacity to manage AVT projects (developing and organizing team projects).

Díaz-Cintas and Remael (2019:57) point out "linguistic competence, sociocultural awareness and subject knowledge are no longer sufficient" in subtitling. Today, subtitlers need to be familiar with state-of-the-art information and communication technologies, demonstrate high technical know-how and quickly adapt to new programs and specifications as they typically work with multiple programs and clients. This may also include the use of ASR/SR and MT for PE subtitles. Thus, when considering the above-mentioned revised PE model and applying it to subtitling, these five subtitling sub competences need to be added to the task and can be visualized as the base of each of the three columns as seen in Figure 2.

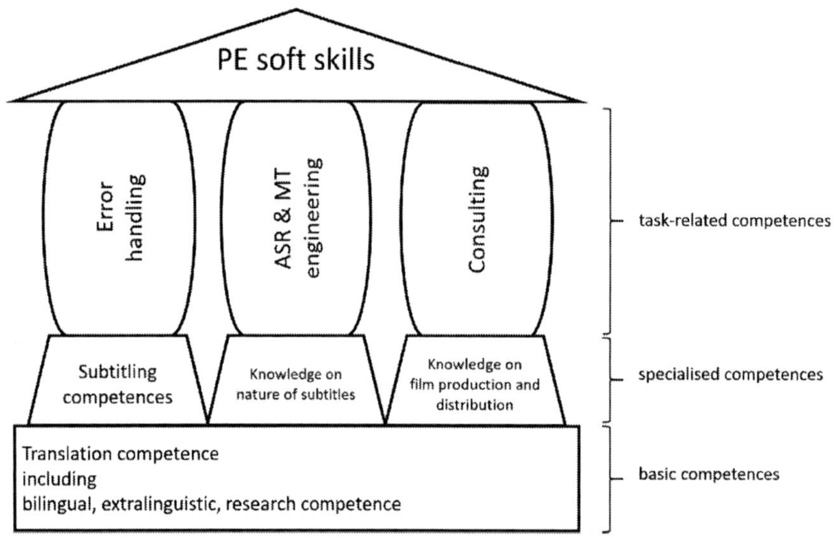

Figure 2 Adjusted model for PE of subtitles.

In general, the model can be split into basic competences (foundation), specialised competences (column bases), and task-related competences (column). Different widths of the columns may express the focus on a specific task and thus help describe possible job profiles as later discussed in Section 3. These tasks require additional soft skills for PE (roof). Besides error handling of the MT output, when post-editing subtitles, the post-editor also needs to be familiar with subtitling-specific competences such as spotting, condensing by analysing image and sound (or audiovisual monitoring), and segmenting longer utterances across lines and subtitles while adhering to the given guidelines, which are far from a world-wide standard. Some of these skills may be less relevant when post-editing in template files, i.e., when the spotting and segmentation of subtitles is already set and translation, or in this case post-editing, is performed within the constraints of the template.

The use of template files is nothing new in subtitling and they may be based on the original intralingual subtitles or on a subtitle file in English as a pivot language (see e.g., Artegiani and Kapsaskis 2014; Nikolić 2015; Georgakopoulou 2019). Subtitle template files can be *verbatim* (word for word, similar to a transcript) and based on automatic subtitles or they can be *sensatim* (meaning for meaning) and thus reduced in nature leaving out words while containing the original meaning (Eugeni and Caro 2019); these are most often human-generated subtitles. Further, template files can be *locked*, with fixed spotting and a set number of subtitles, or *unlocked* with suggested segmentation and timing which can be adjusted by the subtitler or in this case post-editor (Oziemblewska and Szarkowska 2020: 4). When working with pivot template files, the language of the original movie and the pivot template file differs, i.e., a Swedish movie is translated into German via an English template file by a subtitler without knowledge of Swedish. This may have further implications for the profile of the subtitle post-editor. In any case, when source language transcripts, intralingual subtitles or subtitle (pivot) template files are available, MT systems and PE processes can be used on these texts.

An exploratory empirical study by Nitzke (2016) suggests, that PE should not be performed monolingually. The same is particularly true in subtitling and includes not only access to the written words of the source text but also access to the original video. Subtitling is the translation of polysemiotic texts which cannot be isolated from the images and sound in the video. When working with a locked subtitle file, one could argue that access to the original video is not necessary, especially in a pivot setup, when the video is in a language the subtitle post-editor does not understand anyways, and that it would only slow down the process. However, initial results from a study by Tardel (in print) with 13 translation students and 13 professional subtitlers suggests that in PE of movie transcripts via a pivot language the professional subtitlers worked with the video and performed more edits and still they were not significantly slower than students. The students in contrast mainly worked with the written scripts missing the context of the video. This suggests that access to the video is necessary for language-independent information extraction of the audiovisual source text. Here, the mentioned competence of audiovisual monitoring comes into play to support disambiguation during PE.

If no subtitle file or source language transcript is available for MT, SR systems may be used to obtain a transcript in a previous step. This has already been applied in fully automatic setups using automatic speech recognition (ASR) in captioning on YouTube (Alberti and Bacchiani, 2009) and most recently in Google Chrome (Scharff and Kompalli, 2021) with varying quality from language to language and highly depending on the audio quality and speakers in the audiovisual material. YouTube and Google apply this directly to the unedited video and without human PE in the process resulting in verbatim subtitles and spotting which is based on the source language content. For professional subtitling settings, ASR quality control and PE is necessary to meet the respective quality expectations and efficiency gains. When ASR is used in combination with MT, recognition errors from the ASR might be transferred. Thus, post-editors will also have to be familiar with the types of errors generated by ASR systems which includes adjusting errors in automatic timing, compression, and segmentation. Work by Koponen et al. (2020) has shown in a small-scale study that PE of MT subtitles results in faster production with fewer keystrokes, but they point out that segmentation and timing of subtitles play a key role in the process when it comes to quality and production effort. To address this, Matusov et al. (2019) developed and tested a system for customizing NMT to subtitling by including a segmentation algorithm based on subtitle rules such as maximum characters per line and lines per subtitle in relation to the assumed reading speed, as well as punctuation, part-of-speech detection, and dialogue turns. As segmentation in subtitling is often not so straight forward, they trained a neural model for predicting segment boundaries. In their small-scale test with two post-editors, they found improved performance for the adapted MT system over the baseline MT system without the improved automatic segmentation. These developments show that adapting MT for subtitling is essential and its use for PE of subtitles has implications on the expected competences and performance of the subtitler.

In contrast to ASR directly from the audio track of a given video, speaker-dependent SR is being applied in most live-subtitling settings both intralingual and interlingual with respeaking (see e.g., Romero-Fresco, 2020). In contrast to scripted and non-scripted preproduced material, live content is translated into subtitles with a small decalage, similar to interpreting, by means of respeaking (or transpeaking) and simultaneous editing of the SR output. When applying respeaking and PE to preproduced content, similar competences are required as discussed in Pöchhacker and Remael (2019). In preproduced content, however, more focus is put on carful spotting and segmentation. Overlapping competences that are relevant also for post-editing of prepared interlingual subtitles include the technical-methodological competence regarding the speech recognition sub-competences *transpeaking task & process, research and preparation* as well as *editing*.

When editing ASR output – irrespective of trained speaker-dependent SR in respeaking or the direct application of ASR to a video in order to obtain a transcript – the PE subtitler also needs to have an understanding of the applied technology, which errors to expect, and how to correct them most efficiently. Here, the quality of the ASR is crucial in whether it is actually beneficial in the process. Results from a study carried out with video transcripts within the COMPASS project suggest that manual transcription is still preferred and faster when ASR quality is too low (Hansen-Schirra et al., 2020; Tardel, 2020). Similar results were also obtained by Matamala et al. (2017) in a small-case study comparing manual transcription to respeaking and editing ASR. They found the manual transcription yielded the better results compared to ASR and respeaking both regarding temporal effort and quality. Thus, similar to post-editing MT, also the editing of ASR requires competences along the three pillars error handling, ASR engineering and consulting. For applications where ASR produces not the required quality (due to, e.g., low-resource languages, too many speakers, heavy dialects, etc.), respeaking scenarios would also be a possible solution for prepared subtitle productions, giving the subtitler more control over the SR output and allowing the tailoring of the SR system with profiles for similar shows. This, however, has yet to be tested empirically and in realistic workflows.

Before describing three possible job profiles that result from the above-mentioned model in Figure 2, we can conclude that subtitlers working as post-editors of subtitles that are (semi-) automatically generated require fundamental technical-methodological competences regarding MT and SR/ASR including automatic spotting and compression in addition to written translation and post-editing competences and subtitling competences.

3. Job profiles for post-editing subtitles

When MT output is post-edited in the subtitling context, it has implications regarding the necessary competences of the subtitler as well as the respective guidelines and quality expectations. PE for subtitling often not only includes the editing of the machine translated text, but the post-editor also has to time and segment the subtitles. Further, the subtitles must comply with what is shown in the images. Information visible in the image might therefore easily be left out in the subtitles when time and space constraints do not allow for verbatim subtitles. Despite the differences, similar considerations apply to subtitlers and written translators. The job profiles presented in Nitzke and Hansen-Schirra (in press) may be transferred and adapted to AVT settings, in particular interlingual subtitling as visualized in Figure 2.

In the practical post-editing for subtitling profile, a subtitler (or subtitle quality controller, i.e., proofreader) with PE experience performs the PE task. This profile *Subtitle Post-Editor* has also been discussed by Georgakopoulou and Bywood (2014: 27) as well as Bywood et al. (2017: 502). They suggest two options, either the job could be performed by subtitlers with special training in PE or trained post-editors from written translation with special training on subtitling and AVT. Either way, for both the two essential translation competences of the foundation as well as the PE soft skills of the roof apply. The decision who performs the post-editing of subtitles heavily depends on whether the post-editing is performed in a template file (locked or unlocked), on fully automatic subtitles, or with a translated transcript without provided segmentation and timings. In contrast to locked template files more of the subtitling-specific competences are required as this involves spotting, reduction, and segmentation. Thus, besides the aforementioned specific PE skills, post-editors for subtitling need to have knowledge of the client-specific subtitle conventions such as spotting, reduction, segmenting and adjustments from speech to written text as well as matching of the text with the image.

ASR & MT engineers for subtitling need competences regarding system requirement and training processes including approaches for speech processing and language processing. They need the ability to train and assess both ASR and or MT systems in order to perfectly tailor them to the needs of the subtitle post-editor. They therefore need to be aware of the nature of subtitles as synchronized, condensed, and segmented text across lines and subtitles as well as in general of the differences between speech and written text. Further they need to be aware that subtitles may include several languages besides the designated source and target language. Moreover, they need an understanding of different style guides that may depend on the target language, medium, broadcaster or streaming provider. Among others these include subtitle and line length, assumed reading times, and segmentation rules as well as differences in formatting for narrators or forced subs. These could be implemented in customized ASR, MT, and automatic segmentation solutions or at the side of the subtitler when post-editing in the subtitling software that has been configured regarding the specifics of the respective style guide. In addition, engineers need to be aware of different subtitle file formats, availability, and quality of training material (i.e., aligned subtitle files).

A third job profile is *MT consulting for subtitling*, where among others an added understanding of the subtitled media content is required in order to perform the necessary risk management and proper consulting. This includes for movies, knowledge on film rights, genres, and processes of film production and distribution depending whether the content is broadcast on TV, distributed via DVD or online platforms. Subtitled media may also include educational content or subtitles for communication within companies with different impact of quality issues and therefore affecting risk management. Again, translation competences and PE soft skills are essential to grasp the entirety of the task and to best consult language service providers and film producers or distributors alike on when and how to apply MT and PE. This role would be suitable for project managers working in AVT with training on PE.

4. Conclusion

We have shown in this paper that the three suggested PE job profiles can easily be adapted to the subtitling context. Hence, they might also be applicable to other job profiles that make use of MT and PE processes in the translation industry. While adapting the job profiles, the focus has to be on what other competences and knowledge might become relevant and need to be included. Especially when looking at specialized translation settings, the three roles can be adapted with regards to domain-specific translation purposes, but also to more creative text types like marketing or literary translation. Each column of the model can thus be complemented with a base containing specialised knowledge and competences.

Further discussions are needed for the translation of non-scripted audiovisual material. As mentioned, possible solutions include the application of ASR and post-editing of the ASR output. Another avenue could be the application of respeaking and transpeaking, similar to live subtitling, with editing of the improved SR output. After a transcription (manually, semi-automatic with PE of ASR or fully automatic), MT could be used to further translate the content into lower-resource languages via PE. This could be performed on complete transcripts, verbatim or reduced sensatim subtitle template files.

Finally, we propose that the job profiles are implemented in translator training and not as a separate PE add-on afterwards. All three job profiles, both for PE of written texts as well as subtitles, have translation competences at their foundation. Thus, MT engineers and consultants should also have a thorough understanding of translation in order to enter the conversation with the users, i.e., translators and subtitlers. However, it might not be possible to include all necessary aspects of the specialisations in translation curricula as time and capacities are limited and the aim should be to provide modules and trainings for additional competence acquisition.

References

Alberti, C. and Bacchiani M. (2009). Automatic Captioning in YouTube. *Google AI Blog*. Retrieved 10 June 2021 (http://ai.googleblog.com/2009/12/automatic-captioning-in-youtube.html).

Artegiani, I. and Kapsaskis D. (2014). Template Files: Asset or Anathema? A Qualitative Analysis of the Subtitles of The Sopranos. *Perspectives 22*(3):419–36. doi: 10.1080/0907676X.2013.833642.

Bywood, L., Georgakopoulou P. and Etchegoyhen, T. (2017). Embracing the Threat: Machine Translation as a Solution for Subtitling. *Perspectives 25*(3):492–508.

Díaz-Cintas, J. (2020). The Name and Nature of Subtitling. In *The Palgrave Handbook of Audiovisual Translation and Media Accessibility,* pages 149–71, Springer.

Díaz-Cintas, J and Remael, A. (2019). Professional Ecosystem. In *Subtitling: concepts and practices,* pages. 32–63, London/New York: Routledge, Taylor & Francis Group.

EMT Expert Group. (2009). Competences for Professional Translators, Experts in Multilingual and Multimedia Communication. *European Master's in Translation (EMT)*.

Eugeni, C. and Caro, R. B. (2019). The LTA project: Bridging the gap between training and the profession in real-time intralingual subtitling. *Linguistica Antverpiensia New Series: Themes in Translation Studies, 18*:87–100.

Georgakopoulou, P. (2019). Template Files: The Holy Grail of Subtitling. *Journal of Audiovisual Translation 2*(2):137–60.

Georgakopoulou, P and Bywood, L. (2014). MT in Subtitling and the Rising Profile of the Post-Editor. *Multilingual 25*(1):24–28.

Göpferich, S. (2009). Towards a Model of Translation Competence and Its Acquisition: The Longitudinal Study TransComp. In *Behind the Mind: Methods, Models and Results in Translation Process Research*, edited by S. Göpferich, A. L. Jakobsen, and I. M. Mess, pages 11–37, Copenhagen: Samfundslitteratur.

Gottlieb, H. (2005). Multidimensional Translation: Semantics Turned Semiotics. In *Proceedings EU High Level Scientific Conference Series: Multidimensional Translation (MuTra)*. Copenhagen.

Hansen-Schirra, S., Tardel, A., Gutermuth S., Schaeffer, M., Denkel, V. and Hagmann-Schlatterbeck, M. (2020). Computer-Aided Subtitling: Split Attention and Cognitive Effort. In *Translatum nostrum: la traducción y la interpretación en el ámbito especializado*, pages 207–24, Comares.

Koponen, M., Sulubacak, U., Vitikainen, K., & Tiedemann, J. (2020). MT for subtitling: User evaluation of post-editing productivity. *Proceedings of the 22nd Annual Conference of the European Association for Machine Translation*, pages 115–124.

Matamala, A., Romero-Fresco, P. and Daniluk, L. (2017). The Use of Respeaking for the Transcription of Non-Fictional Genres: An Exploratory Study. *InTRAlinea: Online Translation Journal 19*.

Matusov, E., Wilken, P., & Georgakopoulou, Y. (2019). Customizing neural machine translation for subtitling. *Proceedings of the Fourth Conference on Machine Translation* (Volume 1: Research Papers), pages 82–93.

Merchán, B. C. (2018). Audiovisual Translator Training. In *The Routledge handbook of audiovisual translation*, edited by L. Pérez González. London/New York: Routledge, Taylor & Francis Group.

Nikolić, K. (2015). The Pros and Cons of Using Templates in Subtitling. In *Audiovisual Translation in a Global Context*, edited by R. B. Piñero and J. D. Cintas, pages 192–202, London: Palgrave Macmillan UK.

Nitzke, J., Hansen-Schirra, S. and Canfora, C. (2019). Risk Management and Post-Editing Competence. *Journal of Specialised Translation 31*:239–59.

Nitzke, J. and Hansen-Schirra, S. (in press). *A Short Guide to Post-Editing*. Berlin: LangSci Press.

O'Brien, S. (2011). Towards Predicting Post-Editing Productivity. *Machine Translation 25*(3):197–215.

Oziemblewska, M. and Szarkowska, A. (2020). 'The Quality of Templates in Subtitling. A Survey on Current Market Practices and Changing Subtitler Competences'. *Perspectives*. doi: 10.1080/0907676X.2020.1791919.

PACTE. (2003). Building a Translation Competence Model. In *Triangulating Translation: Perspectives in Process-Oriented Research*, edited by F. Alves, pages 43–66, Amsterdam: Benjamins.

Pöchhacker, F. and Remael, A. (2019). New Efforts? A Competence-Oriented Task Analysis of Interlingual Live Subtitling. *Linguistica Antverpiensia, New Series – Themes in Translation Studies 18*.

Robert, I. S., Remael, A. and Ureel J. (2017). Towards a Model of Translation Revision Competence. *The Interpreter and Translator Trainer 11*(1):1–19.

Romero-Fresco, P. (2020). Subtitling through speech recognition: Respeaking. Routledge.

Scharff, E. and Kompalli, M. (2021). Chrome Can Now Caption Audio and Video. *Google – The Keyword*. Retrieved 10 June 2021 (https://blog.google/products/chrome/live-caption-chrome/).

Tardel, A. (2020). Effort in Semi-Automatized Subtitling Processes: Speech Recognition and Experience during Transcription. *Journal of Audiovisual Translation 3*(2). doi: 10.47476/jat.v3i2.2020.131.

Tardel, A. (in print). Measuring Effort in Subprocesses of Subtitling. The Case of Post-editing via Pivot Language. In M. Carl (Ed.), *Explorations in Empirical Translation Process Research*, pages. 81–110). Springer.

Operating a Complex SLT System with Speakers and Human Interpreters

Ondřej Bojar, Vojtěch Srdečný, Rishu Kumar, Otakar Smrž
[surname]@ufal.mff.cuni.cz Charles University, MFF, ÚFAL

Felix Schneider
felix.schneider@kit.edu Karlsruhe Institute of Technology, Germany

Barry Haddow, Phil Williams
bhaddow@ed.ac.uk, pwillia4@inf.ed.ac.uk University of Edinburgh

Chiara Canton
chiara.canton@pervoice.it PerVoice

Abstract

We describe our experience with providing automatic simultaneous spoken language translation for an event with human interpreters. We provide a detailed overview of the systems we use, focusing on their interconnection and the issues it brings. We present our tools to monitor the pipeline and a web application to present the results of our SLT pipeline to the end users. Finally, we discuss various challenges we encountered, their possible solutions and we suggest improvements for future deployments.

1 Introduction

In April 2021, a European international organisation hosted an international congress for its members. While the event was originally planned to be in-person, the COVID-19 pandemic meant that all the foreign participants connected remotely. The event was run in 5 languages (English, German, French, Spanish and Russian) covered by human interpreters. The remote audience spanned 51 countries with the total of 42 desired languages. Our role was to provide live translation into these additional languages in text form.

The technical backstage of the event operated in the standard in-person mode, with interpreters in their booths, following the main live video stream and providing or relaying interpretation as needed. This resulted in six audio channels being available, one for each language and one additional channel called "the floor" which always contained the speech of the current speaker regardless the language. The interpreters delivered their interpretation to the appropriate language-labelled channels. Each of the interpreters was translating either from English to their assigned language, or vice versa. At any given moment, there was thus supposed to be exactly one source of English speech, either directly from the speaker or from one of the interpreters. The channel of the language spoken at the floor at a given point was silent (e.g. the German channel when German was coming from the floor, because the German interpreters' booth was busy providing the English interpretation to the English channel).

While this arrangement caused some technical challenges, it also provided novel opportunities. The first challenge was to concurrently follow all the channels using portable equipment and the second challenge was to direct the correct audio channel to the respective speech processing server. The multiple input languages can make the setup interestingly robust: For example, when the speaker is speaking a non-English language, their speech can be automatically transcribed and then machine-translated to English. At the same time, an interpreter is providing human interpretation into English, which can be in turn processed by the English speech recognition system. We thus have two sources of English text and we can choose the better one, live, bypassing any processing hurdles at any of the paths. Conversely, when the speaker is speaking English, the interpreters will be providing their assigned languages, perhaps captured in better sound conditions or better articulated. These languages can again be automatically transcribed and translated to English, serving as alternative sources if the main speaker is hard to follow for the technology.

The paper is structured as follows: in Section 2, we describe our hardware setup at the backstage. Section 3 provides a complete picture of the processing pipeline from 6 input channels to 42 output languages. Section 4 briefly summarizes the key building blocks, namely the speech recognition (ASR) and machine translation (MT) systems used. These systems were cluster-based, run on premises of the individual research institutes contributing them, connected via the Internet. Section 5 presents our web-based solution for live display of the many translations. Several members of our team were on duty to monitor all the components during the event and only one skilled "system operator" was present in person at the backstage. The operator's experience is provided in Section 6 and some of the monitor tools at his disposal are described in Section 7. Section 8 summarizes the planned improvements of the setup and components and Section 9 concludes the paper.

2 Lightweight Hardware Setup for Multi-Source Speech Processing

Building upon our previous experience with speech processing at live events, we knew that desk space would be a limiting factor and that at most one person would be admitted to take care of the system on site. Aside from providing the translation service for the (remote) participants, we also needed to fully record the session for future analysis. The sound engineers facilitating the event itself did not have any recording equipment suitable for our purposes.

Our final solution consisted of one laptop (Dell Vostro 3583) running Ubuntu 20.04 and two Behringer U-Phoria UMC404HD external USB sound cards, each following up to 4 mono sound channels.

To minimize the risk of losing the recording, the system setup was *primarily* geared towards recording. Throughout the session, two `arecord` tasks were recording raw outputs of each of the external sound cards, producing two 4-channel PCM sound files sampled at 44 kHz.

Any sound processing, be it for monitoring purposes or for the actual speech processing, was based upon these growing files. We avoided touching the software sound devices to prevent any software conflicts during the session.

To monitor the incoming sound of any channel across the two recording devices, we simply followed the most recent additions to the respective file and selected the channel with `ffmpeg`:

```
tail -c0 -f RAW_RECORDING.pcm \
| ffmpeg -y -f s32le -acodec pcm_s32le -r 44100 -ac 4 -i - \
    -map_channel 0.0.DESIRED_CHANNEL ... - 2>/dev/null
```

The added benefit of this file-based access to the live sound was that until the actual session was running, we could easily simulate live session by slowly copying data from a pre-recorded sound to mock "raw recording" file:

```
cat SAVED_4-CHANNEL_RECORDING.pcm \
| pv -L 688K -q | dd obs=16 > SIMULATED_RAW_RECORDING.pcm
```

The `pv` command limits throughput, simulating real-time growth, with the byte rate of 688K determined empirically. The `dd obs=16` ensures that the output file grows in multiples of 16 bytes. When watching the "current" sound with `tail -f`, it is guaranteed that the processing starts aligned to the 4 channels in the file.

Such a simulation proved invaluable esp. immediately before the start of the live event. No tests of the components can ensure that the whole complex ensemble is running and ready for an immediate launch.

3 SLT Pipeline Description

Our "SLT pipeline" consists of ASR and MT systems and various components transforming and transporting data between them. The actual setup – which languages to follow, how to switch among them, which ones to use the source for the final translation – varies across events that we already took part in. Here we focus on the particular setup of the international (remote) congress but our tools allow for a rather flexible configuration of the "wiring".

The inputs to the pipeline are the audio sources: English and the five other languages. English audio is converted to text by an English ASR system, while the other languages are converted to English text by the respective ASR system and a subsequent MT system. There is still some room for system optimization by deploying multilingual ASR systems. For MT, we already make use of multi-linguality (a single system trained to translate from any of a small set of languages into English). To achieve independent processing of each of the input languages, each audio source is processed by a separate ASR and MT system.

The central component of the pipeline is a *selection tool*. Given the multiple variants of inputs (all converted to English text), the operator has the option to dynamically choose which one is currently most suitable for the translation into all the desired target languages, as discussed in Section 6 below.

Then, the chosen English text source is fed to a single one-to-many multi-lingual MT system. In our case, the MT system translates the same input text from English to 41 target languages at once.

Finally, the selected English and all the translations are sent to the web application presenting the outputs to the users (Section 5). It is worth mentioning that depending on the sound channel the user is following, they can observe bigger or smaller delay between the speech and the shown translation. For instance, a German user would most likely follow the German speech, but the automatic German transcript can actually be the result of the German interpreter producing English followed by English ASR and English-to-German MT.

There is a potential for improvement in this setup: for the five other non-English spoken languages, we could present their transcription to the users, instead of displaying the output of the one-to-many MT system. This setup would, however, emburden the system operator even more, because the final outputs of these 5 languages would be running on separate paths with independent risk of a crash, requiring independent monitoring. We thus opted for a more uniform approach which was easier to operate: a single input English translated to all languages at once. If any of the target languages stopped updating, the operator knew that all are affected and vice versa.

See Figure 1 for an overview of the data flow when processing non-English speech.

3.1 Pipeline Technical Details

Individual components of the pipeline, such as the ASR or MT systems are distributed across multiple servers at different sites. This has the primary benefit of "immediate deployment". In other words, research systems (as summarized in Section 4 below) are launched by their authors in the known conditions, so the integration time is limited to implementing a simple

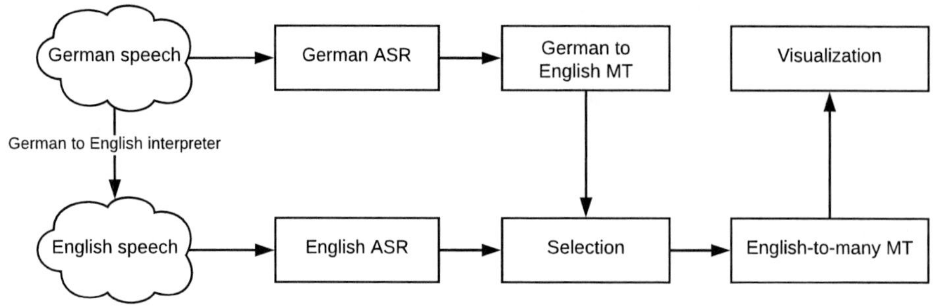

Figure 1: Example of the pipeline when processing German speech.

communication protocol and connecting via TCP connections. Updated models can be included to the pipeline at any point, at their respective author's site and without any involvement of other partners.

Technically, the communication relies on a client-broker service. Individual systems register themselves to the broker, telling the broker what service, e.g. English to German ASR they provide. The broker then publishes a list of available services. Clients then ask the broker for a service and if the service has a provider, the broker facilitates the communication between the client and the service provider. Furthermore, client connectors for audio and text transfer were developed, so the clients can easily send audio and text to the service providers. This setup allows the pipeline operator to pick and choose from various services to integrate into a pipeline, while not having to run all the components locally. A detailed description of the architecture can be found in [Franceschini et al., 2020].

Because the pipelines can grow to be very complex, it was necessary to develop a tool to declaratively describe the pipeline. The pipeline is represented as a directed acyclic graph, with vertices being the individual services, such as English ASR, and edges being the data flow between the services. Each vertex has a set of inputs and outputs, with edges connecting a single output of a vertex to a single input of another vertex. For each particular pipeline, the graph is built in a Python script. The operator describes the vertices and then adds edges between them. Each vertex also contains a command description that starts the component representing the vertex. The command can run fully locally, or it can be the one of the client connectors which passes the task to a remote service offered by the broker. The resulting graph is then compiled to a single bash script which launches all the local commands.

The bash script heavily utilizes network communication on localhost ports to transport the data. The outputs (typically the standard output) of a vertex are captured, replicated and then exposed on different ports. Each output is replicated as many times as there are outgoing edges from that output. Vertices connected to the output then receive one output copy. The splitting is done using standard Unix tools: `tee` that splits the output of a component into multiple subshells, where `netcat` reads it and passes it to another component.

To enable debugging and later reviewing, all standard error outputs of the components are captured and saved to separate files, as well as the edge traffic between individual components. If the captured data are in a plaintext form, each line is also timestamped. This is crucial during analysis of a pipeline failure, as it allows us to deduce what failed and when – if a component fails, the components transitively depending on it usually fail, too.

The local ports are introduced for better process independence. We could in principle directly connect `tee` to the two subsequent components with Unix pipes but in the case of any unexpected exit of any of the components, there would be no way to restart it without restarting the whole pipeline – and also the behaviour of the individual components with respect to the "broken pipe" signal would have to be standardized for predictable behaviour. `netcat` allows us to ensure that the subsequent component's standard input is connected in a stable way and *reopens* the local port upon any failure. This approach is not fully fail-safe but it considerably improves the stability of the whole system.

The compiled bash script can reference many different executables, utilities and files. When multiple people are collaborating on the development of local parts of the pipeline, the deployment can get complicated because everyone has to make sure that various necessary files are being referenced to in a portable way, in addition to the common compilation issues at different systems. Furthermore, these issues are hard to debug, because they are not easily reproducible, unlike e.g. compilation issues.

To alleviate this problem, the bash script is executed inside a Docker container of an image, which already has all of the necessary tools, such as the client connectors or various utilities installed. Another benefit of this approach is a consistent file system structure, allowing to use relative and absolute paths with safety. Similarly, we benefit from the separate network namespace in the Docker container, so ports used for communication between the pipeline components will not collide with ports that the host system might use. While this approach creates some additional technical challenges during development, such as having to rebuild the Docker image when any of the underlying tools is updated, the benefits of having an automatized deployment setup are overall very well worth it.

4 ASR and MT

All ASR systems we used followed the architecture proposed in [Nguyen et al., 2020c] for low-latency online speech recognition. The modeling for all input languages are handled by the streaming sequence-to-sequence model proposed in [Nguyen et al., 2020b] with the use of a multi-domain speech dataset [Nguyen et al., 2020d]. The dynamic transcription mechanism in [Niehues et al., 2016, Nguyen et al., 2020a] is adopted in all ASR systems to achieve very low user-perceived latency.

The MT systems into English are multilingual systems based on the Transformer architecture [Vaswani et al., 2017, Pham et al., 2019]. The system uses a *re-translation* strategy [Niehues et al., 2016] in order to reduce the latency of the MT, as opposed to streaming approaches such as [Ma et al., 2019]. In the re-translation approach, incoming text from ASR is translated afresh starting from the beginning of the sentence, or the end of the stable ASR output, whichever is earlier. Consequently, the new output of the MT system can rewrite, or "flicker" what has already been shown, leading to the question of how best to present this to the user (see Section 5 below). Following [Niehues et al., 2018], we inject partial sentence pairs (prefixes) into the training data so that the system is better able to deal with this at runtime.

Similarly, the one-to-many system that translates out of English is a multilingual Transformer, using the pseudo-word approach to identify the desired language [Johnson et al., 2016]. It is trained on 231M sentence pairs sampled from the OPUS collection [Tiedemann, 2012] and covers 41 target languages, including all official EU languages. The out-of-English systems also use re-translation and prefix training.

To connect ASR and MT, we deploy an NMT-based segmentation component which converts the ASR output (all lower-case, no punctuation, with speech phenomena) into more standardized text by inserting punctuation, inferring capitalization and removing disfluency phenomena [Cho et al., 2012, Cho et al., 2017]. In addition to improving the readability of the transcript, this component is necessary for MT, which is trained to expect orthographically correct (partial) sentences.

5 Presenting Translations

As mentioned above, our ASR systems are gradually *updating* their outputs, not necessarily in the incremental fashion. Similarly, the automatic segmentation can update the placement of punctuation symbols and as a result, the translations from the English-to-many MT systems can and will change over time. This situation (and the problems it brings when the space for the output translation is limited) is thoroughly explained by [Macháček and Bojar, 2020]. In short, there is no easy and non-disturbing solution if an update changes some content which has already been scrolled away due to a small presentation space. Eventually, a translated hypothesis becomes *confirmed*, meaning that the translation is final and will not change any more. While we could simply wait for the translation of a sentence to become confirmed and then display it to the users, it would introduce a needless and sometimes unacceptable delay.

Luckily, our setting allows us to use larger screen space than just the few lines of subtitles as [Macháček and Bojar, 2020] consider. We use the term "paragraph view" for this. Specifically, we developed a web-based interface for presenting the full live transcript of which the tail keeps changing. The web application is hosted on a web server, which receives the translated hypotheses from the MT system. The hypotheses are then published on a websocket, to which the browsers of end users connect. As the browser receives updates and finalized hypotheses from the websocket, it displays them to the end user. Finalized messages are displayed in black and unconfirmed hypotheses are displayed in grey, so the user can distinguish between them.

One important aspect of our setup is the relatively high number of available languages. While the presentation interface is flexible and can accommodate any number of languages, shown as columns, in practice showing too many languages leads to very narrow columns and, subsequently, the text scrolling too fast to be read. Additionally, each user will be interested in following only a very small number of languages and will want them displayed close to each other. A simple table of language codes therefore allows the user to choose which languages get displayed. This choice of languages can also be preloaded by an argument to the tool's URL entrypoint, allowing the event organizers to choose different default languages for different groups of users by spreading different versions of the link.

Based on our experience from several test sessions, we added the option for the operator to *broadcast* messages to users. There are many conditions of operation where some information from the operator would be very valuable for the spectators and would comfort them, such as "the show is delayed, stay tuned", "thank you for watching and we would like some feedback from you", or apologies for the current technical issues etc. We saw in practice that event organizers tend to choose very varied means and platforms of communication with the users, and the attention of users can also wander across them, so it is never certain *where* they would best notice. Broadcasting these messages interleaved with the main content of the transcribed and translated speech is a unifying option here.

It is important to note that these messages have to be delivered in all the supported target languages. To ensure the correctness of these messages, we collected a list of about 20 potentially useful English messages prior to the event. We translated them with our multi-target MT systems and asked many colleagues to review the automatic translations. For a few target languages, no native speaker of the language was available and the automatic translations remained unchecked. Based on the experience at the event, 8 more messages were added, primarily explaining immediate failures or delays that we observed in the *source* stream.

To differentiate them from the translations, these operator messages were displayed in bold. Figure 2 contains an example of the messages displayed to the user.

Figure 2: Example of the hypotheses and operator messages.

6 Operator Experience

The operator was facing a challenging task when the pipeline was running during the live event. He had to monitor all individual parts of the pipeline, spanning from the sound input to the very final presentation in the web interface, and he was also selecting the current best variant of English source for the multi-target translation, as described in more details below.

Because our current pipeline still misses automatic language identification, the operator had one additional task: based on the floor sound which he was constantly following inform the system about any change of the language spoken at the floor. The system was then prepared to redirect "sound pipes" accordingly, so that each of the 5 ASR system inputs always received its language, regardless whether it came from the original speaker (floor) or from an interpreter.

6.1 Noticing Problems

Despite long-term efforts in debugging all the components, some crashes did happen. They can be attributed to unexpected peculiarities of the incoming data and unexpected network conditions, for instance music or video with speech and music played in the main stream. Unexpectedly long silence (e.g. from an interpreter's booth) also occasionally caused the ASR+MT input pipe to timeout and crash.

Crashes are generally easy to spot (if the operator has the screen space and capacity to watch): some outputs become unavailable. What is more difficult to identify is *delay* in processing, e.g. due to some temporary network or system overload. With real interpreters and end-to-end neural ASR systems, a delay in the order of 4 to 7 seconds is the current standard [Macháček et al., 2021]. Noticing that this delay has grown to e.g. 10 or 20 seconds is not easy, esp. considering that there are several such inputs and each of them can suffer the problem individually and to a varying extent. In Section 7, we describe our new means to simplify the task.

6.2 Selecting the Current Best Source

The main responsibility of the operator in our setup was deciding which source of English text will be used as the input to the one-to-many MT system. As described above, there are multiple possible sources of the English text: directly from the speaker or from an interpreter, automatically translated into English as needed.

Each of the possible sources arrives as a sequence of updates. Our processing pipeline uses the automatically predicted punctuation to break it down into "events" aligned with sentence beginnings. An update can lead to multiple events if it contains several sentences in a row. Typically, updates are growing as more input words are recognized and processed, but regularly a "confirmation" update indicates that some history has been finalized and it will no longer appear in the updates. Updates from the different sources are fully independent of each other, with no synchronization at all.

As mentioned above, the subsequent step in the pipeline is the one-to-many MT system, which expects one stream of sentence events.

While we envision many cleverer techniques of input combination, for the described event, the operator was simply choosing which and only which stream on input events should be directed to the one-to-many MT; events from all other streams were discarded during that period.

Technically, each event is a line of text in the pipes. We needed a tool which serves as the `cat` command but allows to choose the source pipe on the fly. For this purpose, a simple Python program was developed. The program consumes an arbitrary number of line-oriented input channels using localhost ports and shows the latest message for each of those outputs to the operator. One of the streams is pre-selected as the default but the operator has the option to signal that for subsequent messages, a different stream should be used. The selection is done by writing the stream identifier to a special file which the program is monitoring.

The user interface for the operator was extremely simplistic for a start: a terminal window running the `watch` command repeatedly monitoring the last few lines of each input. Based on the past events and on the sound from the floor, the operator had to anticipate which input would be most reliable *in the future* events. Due to the asynchronicity of the updates, monitoring the sources was not always easy. What caused a particular problem were large updates that the fully neural ASR tended to make randomly.

At multiple times, the operator experienced a delay in the original English text while the interpreted and translated message was already available. In other words, the double interpretation (e.g. English speaker manually interpreted to French and machine-translated back to English) arrived sooner than the direct English ASR. This can be explained by the interpreter articulating the message to smaller and clearly identifiable chunks, so that the fully neural ASR was confident enough to ship them. With continuous English speech, the ASR was still waiting for a signal of the end of the sentence. Another possible explanation could be some temporary overload at the ASR system. At such occasions, the operator was tempted to (and often did) select some other language as the new source. Sometimes, this was a good choice because the direct English ASR was indeed stuck, but sometimes an update arrived shortly after switching away from that source.

An interesting opportunity to "travel in time" arose from the length of the updates. Sometimes, the operator switched to e.g. the German source because it was more up-to-date at that point. However, after the switch, the original English source was updated and this update covered also a portion of time before the beginning of the already emitted German source. Switching back to the English source thus actually repeated some of the transcribed speech of the current speaker, but worded differently. This situation allowed the operator to occasionally "rewrite" the latest updates, potentially improving the final text for the users. We still want to analyze this situation in a closer detail but improving the technique of input selection and combination is of a higher importance.

6.3 Interesting Specific Cases and Considerations

Live events always bring unexpected situations, beyond what any previous evaluation can cover. For example, one of the remote speakers started presenting in a fully unsupported language, so neither our system nor any of the interpreters knew what to do. This short unexpected silence caused some issues to our components.

Another unexpected situation occurred when a poor Internet connection distorted the speech of one of the (remote) speakers to the point where the interpreters refused to interpret it altogether. However, our English ASR systems were still able to process the audio, so for a short while our SLT service was actually the only source of translated speech. It surely suffered from recognition errors, but it was better than nothing.

We described most of the benefits and problems of the setup above. We have the recording and detailed logs from the event and the permission to use them for a limited period of time. Portions of the recording which do not contain any confidential information will be released later, when the event organizers finish the manual check for confidentiality. When the publishable subset of data is selected, we plan a rigorous evaluation. We want to assess the true extent to which the alternative sources could have helped in producing better outputs and what the operator should have seen and noticed when selecting them. It is also likely that some translations were better for one source while for others, a different source should have been followed instead. Evaluating this aspect is even trickier: using standard reference-based evaluation methods cannot work because different sources lead to different reference translations and comparing scores across different translations is not possible.

6.4 User Feedback

During the event, we distributed a form for the users of the SLT system using operator broadcasting, mentioned in Section 5. Sadly, we received only three responses. Two users were using the SLT system all the time, reporting they preferred quicker, partial translations rather than slower, but more accurate translations. They indicated they would prefer subtitles over the paragraph view described in Section 5, but they were unaware of the problems the limited space of the subtitles brings.

The explicitly mentioned issues were too much text to read and distracting or laughable words. This calls for an improvement not only in terms of recognition and translation quality but also for some text condensation.

7 Pipeline Monitoring Tools

The pipeline is complex and consists of many separate components. It can be only expected that something will break, sooner or later. Thus, a set of tools monitoring the health and status of the pipeline was developed. Coming back to the pipeline representation as a directed acyclic graph, it makes sense to monitor two parts of the graph structure: the health of individual components (vertices) and the data flow between them (edges).

To monitor the individual components, the pipeline (as compiled to the bash script) saves (UNIX) process IDs of all the components. Then, a simple script regularly checks if processes with these IDs are still running, showing the status of each component to the operator. This allows for cursory checks of which components of the pipeline, e.g. a client connected to an ASR system, are up and running and which components have fully broken down.

Similarly, all intermediate component outputs and standard error outputs are duplicated to separate files via a modified `tee` which adds exact timestamps at the beginning of each saved line. This detailed (and now fully automated) logging proved essential both during the development as well as during the live event. These logs are recorded only on the operator's machine but it proved very useful to regularly upload them to a shared space where all technical team members could help investigating what is going on because the operator is generally fully occupied with other tasks. We are aware that there are server-based logging solutions but our approach is flexible, lightweight and does not need any external tools.

In debugging, absolute timestamps in the logs are necessary when investigating why the pipeline crashed. This usually involves cross-checking many logs and timestamps are the best means of finding the culprit. In several occasions, we also made use of these timestamped logs to replay some problematic input, allowing us to debug only one isolated component.

During live deployments, these log files are also monitored. The simplest approach taken at the reported event is to `tail -F` all the standard error outputs at once to see the latest errors of any component.

For the intermediate output files (i.e. the data that are passed along each of the pipeline graph edge) we developed a new tool. This tool tracks the moving average of the time between output updates (simply checking for changes in log modification time). Whenever the average extension time elapses with a suitable margin but no output is added, the operator is notified. This is a very flexible detection of situations where the components are running, but for some reason they stop or slow down outputting data.

8 Future Improvements

Although the event went quite smoothly for us and there were no major technical issues or hiccups, we discovered some sore points and opportunities to improve. First, the task of the operator is quite demanding, as they have to constantly monitor the state of the pipeline, select the currently best-performing English text source and broadcast operator messages to the end users when necessary.

While the operator already has some tools to monitor the health of the pipeline, they still have to juggle multiple monitoring tools. To alleviate this, we propose to use a web application as the control center for the operator. The server for the web application would live in the Docker container, as described in Section 3.1, along with the pipeline and it would provide an API to obtain the last few lines of each stored-output file, list of running processes and other necessary information. The operator would then be able to simply observe and control the pipeline in their web browser.

Another improvement could be automatically switching the English text source input of the English-to-many MT system based on ASR confidence levels and other criteria. This would free the operator from having to constantly monitor the English text sources and judge which one is currently performing the best. However, the definition of these criteria would not be straightforward due to the different nature (and possible means of confidence estimation) of the components.

The operator messages were pre-translated before the event and revised for quality. A nice addition would be the option to simply type a new operator message in English, let that sentence be translated by the English-to-many MT system and then broadcast it to the end users.

9 Conclusion

We described our experience with running a complex system for spoken language translation aimed at substantially extending the set of provided target languages. From five official languages of the event, provided by human interpreters, we were able to cover 42 languages spoken in the participant's countries.

We proposed a novel technique increasing the overall robustness of the system to technical or human failures, namely following multiple sources at once and dynamically choosing the current best one. While the technique was so far tested in its simplest form, switching between the sources manually, it helped us to navigate through partial system failures. At one occasion, our system was the only translation service available, because even human interpreters have given up processing the sound from a distorted remote call.

For the future, we plan to improve the user interface for the operator. Any means of automatic diagnostics, incl. recognition and translation confidence, would be highly desirable. We will also focus on more advanced techniques for combining multiple inputs.

Acknowledgements

This work has received funding from the European Union's Horizon 2020 Research and Innovation Programme under Grant Agreements No 825460 (ELITR).

References

[Cho et al., 2012] Cho, E., Niehues, J., and Waibel, A. (2012). Segmentation and punctuation prediction in speech language translation using a monolingual translation system. In *IWSLT 2012*.

[Cho et al., 2017] Cho, E., Niehues, J., and Waibel, A. (2017). Nmt-based segmentation and punctuation insertion for real-time spoken language translation. In *Interspeech 2017*.

[Franceschini et al., 2020] Franceschini, D., Canton, C., Simonini, I., Schweinfurth, A., Glott, A., Stüker, S., Nguyen, T.-S., Schneider, F., Ha, T.-L., Waibel, A., Haddow, B., Williams, P., Sennrich, R., Bojar, O., Sagar, S., Macháček, D., and Smrž, O. (2020). Removing European language barriers with innovative machine translation technology. In *Proceedings of the 1st International Workshop on Language Technology Platforms*, pages 44–49, Marseille, France. European Language Resources Association.

[Johnson et al., 2016] Johnson, M., Schuster, M., Le, Q. V., Krikun, M., Wu, Y., Chen, Z., Thorat, N., Viégas, F., Wattenberg, M., Corrado, G., Hughes, M., and Dean, J. (2016). Google's Multilingual Neural Machine Translation System: Enabling Zero-Shot Translation. *ArXiv e-prints*.

[Ma et al., 2019] Ma, M., Huang, L., Xiong, H., Zheng, R., Liu, K., Zheng, B., Zhang, C., He, Z., Liu, H., Li, X., Wu, H., and Wang, H. (2019). STACL: Simultaneous Translation with Implicit Anticipation and Controllable Latency using Prefix-to-Prefix Framework. In *Proceedings of the 57th Annual Meeting of the Association for Computational Linguistics*, pages 3025–3036, Florence, Italy. Association for Computational Linguistics.

[Macháček and Bojar, 2020] Macháček, D. and Bojar, O. (2020). Presenting simultaneous translation in limited space. In *Proceedings of the 20th Conference Information Technologies - Applications and Theory (ITAT 2020)*, pages 32–37, Košice, Slovakia. Tomáš Horváth.

[Macháček et al., 2021] Macháček, D., Žilinec, M., and Bojar, O. (2021). Lost in interpreting: Speech translation from source or interpreter? In *Interspeech 2021, 22nd Annual Conference of the International Speech Communication Association*. ISCA.

[Nguyen et al., 2020a] Nguyen, T. S., Niehues, J., Cho, E., Ha, T.-L., Kilgour, K., Muller, M., Sperber, M., Stueker, S., and Waibel, A. (2020a). Low latency asr for simultaneous speech translation. *arXiv preprint arXiv:2003.09891*.

[Nguyen et al., 2020b] Nguyen, T.-S., Pham, N.-Q., Stüker, S., and Waibel, A. (2020b). High performance sequence-to-sequence model for streaming speech recognition. *Proc. Interspeech 2020*, pages 2147–2151.

[Nguyen et al., 2020c] Nguyen, T.-S., Stueker, S., and Waibel, A. (2020c). Super-human performance in online low-latency recognition of conversational speech. *arXiv preprint arXiv:2010.03449*.

[Nguyen et al., 2020d] Nguyen, T.-S., Stüker, S., and Waibel, A. (2020d). Toward cross-domain speech recognition with end-to-end models. *arXiv preprint arXiv:2003.04194*.

[Niehues et al., 2016] Niehues, J., Nguyen, T. S., Cho, E., Ha, T.-L., Kilgour, K., Müller, M., Sperber, M., Stüker, S., and Waibel, A. (2016). Dynamic transcription for low-latency speech translation. In *Interspeech 2016*, pages 2513–2517.

[Niehues et al., 2018] Niehues, J., Pham, N.-Q., Ha, T.-L., Sperber, M., and Waibel, A. (2018). Low-Latency Neural Speech Translation. In *Proceedings of Interspeech 2018*.

[Pham et al., 2019] Pham, N.-Q., Nguyen, T.-S., Ha, T.-L., Hussain, J., Schneider, F., Niehues, J., Stüker, S., and Waibel, A. (2019). The iwslt 2019 kit speech translation system. In *Proceedings of IWSLT 2019*.

[Tiedemann, 2012] Tiedemann, J. (2012). Parallel data, tools and interfaces in opus. In Chair), N. C. C., Choukri, K., Declerck, T., Dogan, M. U., Maegaard, B., Mariani, J., Odijk, J., and Piperidis, S., editors, *Proceedings of the Eight International Conference on Language Resources and Evaluation (LREC'12)*, Istanbul, Turkey. European Language Resources Association (ELRA).

[Vaswani et al., 2017] Vaswani, A., Shazeer, N., Parmar, N., Uszkoreit, J., Jones, L., Gomez, A. N., Kaiser, Ł., and Polosukhin, I. (2017). Attention is all you need. *Advances in Neural Information Processing Systems*, 30:5998–6008.

Simultaneous Speech Translation for Live Subtitling: from Delay to Display

Alina Karakanta *♪♩ akarakanta@fbk.eu
Sara Papi *♪♩ spapi@fbk.eu
Matteo Negri ♪ negri@fbk.eu
Marco Turchi ♪ turchi@fbk.eu
♪ Fondazione Bruno Kessler, Via Sommarive 18, Povo, Trento, Italy
♩ University of Trento, Italy

Abstract

With the increased audiovisualisation of communication, the need for live subtitles in multilingual events is more relevant than ever. In an attempt to automatise the process, we aim at exploring the feasibility of simultaneous speech translation (SimulST) for live subtitling. However, the word-for-word rate of generation of SimulST systems is not optimal for displaying the subtitles in a comprehensible and readable way. In this work, we adapt SimulST systems to predict subtitle breaks along with the translation. We then propose a display mode that exploits the predicted break structure by presenting the subtitles in scrolling lines. We compare our proposed mode with a display 1) word-for-word and 2) in blocks, in terms of reading speed and delay. Experiments on three language pairs (en→it, de, fr) show that scrolling lines is the only mode achieving an acceptable reading speed while keeping delay close to a 4-second threshold. We argue that simultaneous translation for readable live subtitles still faces challenges, the main one being poor translation quality, and propose directions for steering future research.

1 Introduction

The globalisation of business, education and entertainment, together with the recent movement restrictions, have transferred human interaction to the online sphere. The boom in online multilingual communication is setting new challenges for achieving barrierless interaction between audiences with diverse linguistic and accessibility needs. Subtitles, as a key means for ensuring accessibility, have been adapted to respond to the challenge of timely communication, giving rise to live subtitling. Live subtitling, whether intralingual (same language as the speech) or interlingual (different language than the speech), allows for obtaining subtitles in real time and is recently witnessing an upsurging demand in a range of occasions; from news and TV programmes, to online meetings, conferences, live events, shows and university lectures, live subtitles are bringing the world closer together.

Technology has always been a leading factor in live subtitling. Live subtitles were initially obtained by means of keyboards or stenotyping, but Automatic Speech Recognition (ASR) gave rise to respeaking, a technique where the subtitler respeaks the original sound into an ASR system, which produces the subtitles on the screen (Romero-Fresco, 2011). Although originally employed for intralingual subtitles, respeaking is gradually extending to produce interlingual subtitles, a task bearing close resemblance to simultaneous interpreting. Still, the tediousness

*Equal contribution

of the task and the scarcity of highly-skilled professionals for live subtitling call for a more pronounced role of technology for providing real-time access to information.

These growing needs for access to multilingual spoken content have motivated researchers to develop fully automatic solutions for real-time spoken language translation (Grissom II et al., 2014; Gu et al., 2017; Alinejad et al., 2018; Arivazhagan et al., 2019; Ma et al., 2019). The new possibilities opened up by neural machine translation have led to improvements in automatic simultaneous speech-to-text translation (SimulST). In SimulST (Ma et al., 2020; Ren et al., 2020), the generation of the translation starts before the entire audio input is received, which is an indispensable characteristic for achieving low latency (translation delay) between speech and text in live events. The translation becomes available at consecutive steps, usually one word at a time. However, a display mode based on the word-for-word rate of generation of SimulST systems may not be optimal for displaying readable subtitles. Studies in intralingual subtitling have shown that a word-for-word display increases the number of saccadic crossovers between text and scene (Rajendran et al., 2013) and leaves viewers less time to look at the images (Romero-Fresco, 2010). For this reason, regulators, such as the UK Office of Communications, recommended displaying subtitles in blocks (Ofcom, 2015). However, this display mode is not ideal for live events since waiting until the block is filled before displaying the subtitle would extremely increase latency at the risk of losing synchronisation with the speaker. Despite the existence of some applications of SimulST, so far no work has explored its potential for live subtitling and how the delay in generation impacts the readability of the subtitles.

Given the boosting demand in live subtitles and previous studies on the readability of live subtitles, in this work we pose the following research questions: **1) Can automatic simultaneous translation be a viable method for producing live interlingual subtitles? 2) What are the challenges of the generation mode of SimulST systems for the readability of the subtitles?** We first explore the performance of a direct SimulST system on three language pairs (en→it, de, fr) in terms of translation quality and its ability of generating readable subtitles in terms of technical constraints, such as length and proper segmentation. Second, we investigate two methods for displaying live subtitles, i.e. i) word-for-word and ii) blocks, and how the display mode affects their readability (reading speed and delay). Thirdly, we propose scrolling lines, a mixed display method which takes advantage of the ability of our system to define proper line breaks and show that it leads to a more comfortable reading speed at an acceptable delay. Lastly, we discuss challenges and recommendations for applying simultaneous translation for live subtitling.

2 Related work

2.1 Live subtitling and its reception

Live subtitles are a simpler and more customisable alternative to other ways of translating speech, such as simultaneous interpreting (Marsh, 2004). Originally, the practice of live subtitling was used to produce intralingual subtitles, in order to enable deaf or hard-of-hearing persons to follow live TV programs (Lambourne, 2006). With the widening definition of accessibility beyond the deaf and hard-of-hearing to include persons not speaking the source speech language, live subtitling was adapted to provide interlingual subtitles (Dawson, 2019).

Live subtitles were produced initially with standard keyboards, but the need to reduce latency led to resorting to stenography or to the invention of a customised syllabic keyboard, called Velotype[1]. With the adoption of ASR technologies, respeaking became the most popular technique for live subtitling (Lambourne, 2006). With this technique, a respeaker listens to the original sound of a (live) event and respeaks it to an ASR software, which turns the recog-

[1]https://www.velotype.com/en/homepage-eng/

nized utterances into subtitles (Romero-Fresco 2011). In its interlingual mode, live subtitling is a newly established practice and therefore the industry is experimenting with different profiles for the role of interlingual live subtitlers (Pöchhacker and Remael, 2020). Interlingual live subtitling requires skills from three disciplines: respeaking, subtitling and simultaneous interpreting. As a result, the availability of highly-skilled professionals for interlingual live subtitling cannot meet the growing needs in real-time multilingual communication.

Except for the quality of live subtitles, their speed and display mode greatly affect the user's views, perception and comprehension (Perego et al., 2010). The faster the subtitles, the more time users spend on reading them, and therefore they have less time to focus on the images, which negatively impacts comprehension. Recommendations for comfortable reading speed depend on the user group and language. For example, 15 characters per second (cps) are recommended for live interlingual English SDH – subtitles for the deaf and hard of hearing – (Ofcom, 2005), 12-15 cps for offline interlingual subtitling in Central Europe (Szarkowska, 2016), 17–20 cps in global online streaming services (Netflix, 2021) and 21 cps for TED Talks (TED, 2021). According to Romero-Fresco (2015), a fast subtitle speed of 17–18 cps allows viewers to spend approximately 80% time on subtitles and only 20% on images. As for the display mode, Romero-Fresco (2010) found that a word-for-word display results in viewers spending 90% of time reading the subtitles as opposed to 10% looking at the images, which detriments comprehension. Moreover, the presence of the word to the right of fixation is vital for fluent reading (Rayner et al., 2006) and its absence leads to more re-reading (Sharmin et al., 2016). Rajendran et al. (2013) showed that scrolling subtitles cause the viewers to spend significantly more time reading than subtitles appearing in blocks. These findings have been assumed by broadcasters in several countries to replace their scrolling subtitles by block subtitles where possible. Currently, a word-for-word display is used in most live speech translation applications, such as STACL (Ma et al., 2019), ELITR (Bojar et al., 2021) and Google Translate (Arivazhagan et al., 2020). In this work, we experiment with displaying the output of SimulST systems in ways which turn out to be more comfortable for the viewer, leading to better comprehension and a more pleasant user experience.

2.2 Simultaneous translation

Simultaneous Speech Translation (SimulST) is the task in which the generation of the translation starts before the audio input becomes entirely available. In simultaneous settings, a model has to choose, at each time step, a read or a write action, that is, whether to receive new information from the input or to write using the information received until that step. Consequently, a SimulST system needs a policy which decides the next action. Decision policies can be divided into: *fixed*, when the decision is taken based on the elapsed time, and *adaptive*, when the decision is taken by looking also at the contextual information extracted from the input. Even if the adoption of a fixed policy disregards the input context leading to a sub-optimal solution, little research has been done on adaptive policies (Gu et al., 2017; Zheng et al., 2019a, 2020) because they are hard and time-consuming to train (Zheng et al., 2019b; Arivazhagan et al., 2019).

Among the fixed policies, the most popular and recently studied is the wait-k strategy, which was first proposed by Ma et al. (2019) for simultaneous Machine Translation (SimulMT). The SimulMT wait-k policy is based on waiting for k source words before starting to generate the target sentence. This simple yet effective approach was then employed in SimulST, as in Ma et al. (2020) and Ren et al. (2020), by using direct models i.e. models that, given an audio source, generate a textual target without the need for intermediate transcription steps.

While the original wait-k implementation is based on textual source data, Ma et al. (2020) adapted this strategy to the audio domain by waiting for k fixed amount of time (step size) instead of k words. The best step size resulting from their experiments was 280ms, corresponding to, approximately, the length of a word – on average 271ms – motivating the equivalence between the MT and the ST policies. In Ren et al. (2020), the adaptation was done differently since their direct system includes a segmentation module that is able to determine word boundaries i.e. when a word finishes and the successive one starts. In this case, the wait-k strategy is applied by waiting for k pauses which are automatically detected by the segmenter.

Some studies have attempted to improve the performance of the wait-k strategy, both in relation to latency and quality. For instance, Nguyen et al. (2021) propose to emit more than one token during the writing mode to improve the quality-latency trade-off, while Elbayad et al. (2020) propose a unidirectional encoder instead of a standard SimulST bidirectional encoder (i.e. avoiding to update the encoder states after each READ action) to slow down the decoding phase. However, these systems are not applicable in our case since Nguyen et al. (2021) uses an offline system which is simulated as a simultaneous system during the decoding phase while the model of Elbayad et al. (2020) is for SimulMT and not for SimulST. No previous work has explored the possibilities offered by SimulST for the generation of live subtitles.

3 SimulST for live subtitling

3.1 Simultaneous ST models

The SimulST systems used in this work are based on direct ST models (Bérard et al., 2016; Weiss et al., 2017), which are composed of an audio encoder and a text decoder. The encoder starts from the audio features extracted from the input signal and computes a hidden representation, while the decoder transforms this representation into the target text. These systems have been shown to have lower latency (Ren et al., 2020) – an important factor in simultaneous systems – compared to cascade systems, which perform two generation steps, one for transcription and one for translation. Moreover, Karakanta et al. (2020a) suggested that direct ST systems, having access to the audio source, make better subtitle segmentation decisions by taking advantage of the pauses in the audio.

In order to adapt SimulST systems for the task of live interlingual subtitling, we force the system to learn from human subtitle segmentation decisions by training on data annotated with break symbols which correspond to subtitle breaks (`<eob>` for end of a subtitle block and `<eol>` for end of line inside a subtitle block). These break symbols, if positioned properly, are the key element which allows us to experiment with different display modes for live subtitles.

Our direct SimulST models combine the efficiency of the wait-k strategy (Ma et al., 2019) and the findings of Karakanta et al. (2020a) for obtaining readable subtitles with direct ST systems. This decision policy was also chosen because it allows us to control the latency of our systems. In this way, we can study the effect of latency both on the conformity of the subtitles and on the subtitle display modes.

3.2 Display modes

We experiment with the following three display modes: 1) word-for-word, 2) blocks, and 3) scrolling lines. Figure 1 shows an example of a subtitle displayed in the different modes.

Word-for-word: In the word-for-word display, words appear sequentially on the screen as soon as they are generated by the system. One line at the bottom of the screen is filled from left to right until no more space is available on the right. Then, the line disappears and a new line is filled again. As already mentioned, this display mode is used in most simultaneous applications and follows the generation process of the SimulST system. Naturally, the length of the subtitle depends on the size of the screen. In our case, we selected a maximum of 84 characters, which matches the max. length of a full subtitle block of the block method (see

step	Word-for-word	Blocks	Scrolling lines
In	In		
alcuni	In alcuni		
casi	In alcuni casi		
è	In alcuni casi è		
perché	In alcuni casi è perché		
non	In alcuni casi è perché non		
sono	In alcuni casi è perché non sono		
adatti	In alcuni casi è perché non sono adatti		
<eob>	In alcuni casi è perché non sono adatti	In alcuni casi è perché non sono adatti	In alcuni casi è perché non sono adatti
o	In alcuni casi è perché non sono adatti o	In alcuni casi è perché non sono adatti	In alcuni casi è perché non sono adatti
non	In alcuni casi è perché non sono adatti o non	In alcuni casi è perché non sono adatti	In alcuni casi è perché non sono adatti
hanno	In alcuni casi è perché non sono adatti o non hanno	In alcuni casi è perché non sono adatti	In alcuni casi è perché non sono adatti
etica,	In alcuni casi è perché non sono adatti o non hanno etica,	In alcuni casi è perché non sono adatti	In alcuni casi è perché non sono adatti
<eob>	In alcuni casi è perché non sono adatti o non hanno etica,	o non hanno etica,	In alcuni casi è perché non sono adatti o non hanno etica,
ma	In alcuni casi è perché non sono adatti o non hanno etica, ma	o non hanno etica,	In alcuni casi è perché non sono adatti o non hanno etica,
spesso,	In alcuni casi è perché non sono adatti o non hanno etica, ma spesso	o non hanno etica,	In alcuni casi è perché non sono adatti o non hanno etica,
ci	In alcuni casi è perché non sono adatti o non hanno etica, ma spesso ci	o non hanno etica,	In alcuni casi è perché non sono adatti o non hanno etica,
hanno	In alcuni casi è perché non sono adatti o non hanno etica, ma spesso ci hanno	o non hanno etica,	In alcuni casi è perché non sono adatti o non hanno etica,
condotto	condotto	o non hanno etica,	In alcuni casi è perché non sono adatti o non hanno etica,
<eol>	condotto	o non hanno etica,	o non hanno etica, ma spesso, ci hanno condotto
a	condotto a	o non hanno etica,	o non hanno etica, ma spesso, ci hanno condotto
obiettivi	condotto a obiettivi	o non hanno etica,	o non hanno etica, ma spesso, ci hanno condotto
sbagliati.	condotto a obiettivi sbagliati.	o non hanno etica,	o non hanno etica, ma spesso, ci hanno condotto
<eob>	condotto a obiettivi sbagliati.	ma spesso, ci hanno condotto a obiettivi sbagliati.	ma spesso, ci hanno condotto a obiettivi sbagliati.

Figure 1: Example sentence displayed in the three different modes. Words on the left column correspond to the time steps.

below) [2] and approximates the length observed in the STACL demo.[3]

Blocks: In this mode, the subtitles are displayed only when a full subtitle block is completed. This means that the system continues generating words which are only displayed when the block delimiter <eob> is generated. The subtitle block remains on screen until the next <eob> symbol is generated, therefore the first subtitle is substituted by the next one. Display in blocks is used primarily in offline subtitling, where subtitles are prepared beforehand.

Scrolling lines: Instead of waiting for the full block, we propose a mode in which each line is displayed as soon as a break is predicted (either <eob> or <eol>). Whenever a new break is predicted, the previous line moves to the upper row of the block and the new line occupies the lower row. Since the allowed number of lines in a block is two, each line moves from the lower to the upper row before disappearing. This mode combines the benefits of the two previous methods. It reduces the dynamicity of the text compared to the word-for-word display, it makes content available earlier than the block display, it allows for access to extended context and it reduces long-distance eye movements since the previous line appears above. This mode is similar to the most popular mode employed for broadcasting, with the difference that there is no word-for-word display inside the lines.

The last two display modes are possible because of the ability of our SimulST system to predict subtitle breaks, which was not considered before in SimulST.

3.3 Evaluation of display modes

Our evaluation of the generated subtitles follows Ofcom's recommendations (Ofcom, 2015) and focuses on three key dimensions: quality, delay between utterance and subtitle, and reading

[2] According to the TED Talk subtitling guidelines.

[3] https://simultrans-demo.github.io/

speed. For the display modes the quality is fixed, since they are applied to the same output. We thus focus on the speed and delay. In general, the reading speed is computed in characters per second (cps), as the number of characters over the total time of display. A low but also constant reading speed is pivotal for user experience, considering that it represents how fast or slow a user has to read. Since each of the display methods described in Section 3.2 has a different granularity, the computation of the reading speed has to take into account these visualization differences. The computations of reading speed and delay are described in detail for each visualization mode below.[4]

Reading Speed. In the **Word-for-word** mode (see Figure 1) a word appears on screen as soon as it is generated and remains on screen until the block changes, i.e. when the 84-character limit is reached. Thus, the amount of time available for a user to read this word and all the following words of the block – hereinafter display time – is the interval elapsed from the generation of the word to that of the first word of the successive block. Consequently, the reading speed can be computed at each generation step as the length (in characters) of the generated word and of the successive words of the block divided by the display time. After computing the reading speed for each word of a block, the block-level reading speed is obtained by taking the maximum value since this represents how fast a user has to read to avoid losing part of the text.

Formally, each block corresponds to a group of words of maximum 84 characters or to the last group of words before end of sentence (`<eos>`) is emitted, i.e. the end of the audio segment. Thus, a block is composed by a set of W words $w_1, ..., w_W$ emitted at times $t_1, ..., t_W$, measured in seconds. At time t_{W+1}, the successive block starts or `<eos>` is emitted.

With this notation, we can compute the reading speed as follows:

$$rs = \max_{i=1,\dots,W} \frac{len(text_i)}{elapsed_i} \tag{1}$$

where:

$$elapsed_i = \begin{cases} \texttt{DELAY\_K}, & w_i = \texttt{<eos>} \\ t_{i+1} - t_i, & i = W \\ t_{i+1} - t_i + elapsed_{i+1}, & otherwise \end{cases} \tag{2}$$

$$text_i = \begin{cases} w_i & i = W \\ w_i + \texttt{SPACE} + text_{i+1} & otherwise \end{cases} \tag{3}$$

and `SPACE` represents a blank space added between the two texts. If the block is the last block of the audio segment, we do not know the emission time of the next word. For this reason, we use a fictitious delay:

$$\texttt{DELAY\_K} = 0.280s \cdot k$$

where k corresponds to the k of the wait-k policy. This amount of time is a lower bound for the generation time of the first token of the next segment. As the wait-k policy reads for k steps (each of them lasting 280ms) and then generates the first word, the actual elapsed time will always be higher as it includes the time required for the generation of the word. Thus, `DELAY_K` represents a conservative estimation of the time available to read the last word.

For the **Blocks** mode, the block/line structure of the subtitles is exploited and a block stays on screen until the next block is filled. The reading speed is computed at block level, dividing its length by the time elapsed between the display time of the current block and that of the successive one. In an audio segment with B blocks, each block b is composed by W_b words

[4]The code is available at: `https://github.com/sarapapi/reading_speed`

$w_1, .., w_{W_b}$, where w_{W_b} is the <eob> . Each word w_i is emitted at time t_i, thus each block b is emitted at time t_{W_b}, hereinafter t_b. Using this notation, Equations 2 and 3 become:

$$elapsed_b = \begin{cases} \texttt{DELAY\_K}, & b = B \\ t_{b+1} - t_b, & otherwise \end{cases} \tag{4}$$

$$text_b = \sum_{i=1}^{W_b - 1} \begin{cases} \texttt{BLANK}, & w_i = \texttt{<eol>} \\ w_i, & i = W_b - 1 \\ w_i + \texttt{SPACE}, & otherwise \end{cases} \tag{5}$$

where BLANK corresponds to the empty string and, as before, DELAY_K conservatively accounts for the last unknown block time. In $text_b$ we do not consider <eol> and <eob> (the W_b-th word) for the reading speed computation since they are only used for formatting the subtitles and are not read by the user. Consequently, the reading speed of a block is:

$$rs = \frac{len(text_b)}{elapsed_b} \tag{6}$$

Our proposed display mode, **Scrolling Lines**, also exploits the subtitle structure considering both <eob> and <eol> as a unique <eol> delimiter. Since each line scrolls up when another is generated and two lines stay together on the screen, each line is displayed until the next two lines are generated. As a consequence, the reading speed is computed at line level, dividing the length of a line by the time needed to generate the two successive lines.

If we denote L as the number of lines present in an audio segment, then each line l is composed by W_l words $w_1, .., w_{W_l}$ emitted at times $t_1, ..., t_{W_l}$, where w_{W_l} is the <eol> and $t_{W_l} = t_l$ is its emission time. In this case, the reading speed is calculated at line-level instead of block-level, considering that each line is displayed until the next two lines (since a block can be composed by two lines) are produced. Thus, Equations 4, 5 and 6 are modified as follows:

$$rs = \frac{len(text_l)}{elapsed_l} \tag{7}$$

$$elapsed_l = \begin{cases} \texttt{DELAY\_K}, & l = L \\ (t_{l+2} - t_{l+1}) + (t_{l+1} - t_l), & otherwise \end{cases} \tag{8}$$

$$text_l = \sum_{i=1}^{W_l - 1} \begin{cases} w_i, & i = W_l - 1 \\ w_i + \texttt{SPACE}, & otherwise \end{cases} \tag{9}$$

where, in this case, DELAY_K conservatively accounts for the last unknown line time.

Delay. The delay is estimated as the time between speech and subtitling. While in intralingual subtitling the correspondence between audio and subtitle is easier to establish, the interlingual setting poses the challenge of finding the correspondences between source audio and target text. Since a word-aligner would capture semantic correspondences, we opt for a temporal-based correspondence, based on the system's lagging. Therefore delay is calculated as:

$$delay = \sum_{i=1}^{w_i} (t\_display_w - t\_received_w - \texttt{DELAY\_K}) \tag{10}$$

where $t\_display_w$ is the time the word was displayed on screen and $t\_received_w$ the utterance time corresponding to the displayed token, minus the k-wait delay. For word-for-word display, the time of display corresponds to the system's elapsed time, therefore the delay equals the system's lagging. For block and scrolling lines display, the time of display is the time elapsed for the generation of the break (<eob> for blocks or any break for scrolling lines).

4 Experimental setting

Data For our experiments we use MuST-Cinema (Karakanta et al., 2020b), an ST corpus compiled from TED Talk subtitles. This corpus is ideal for exploring display modes other than word-for-word because it contains subtitle breaks as special symbols. We conduct experiments on three language pairs, English→Italian (442 hours), English→German (408 hours) and English→French (492 hours). For tuning and evaluation we use the MuST-Cinema dev and test sets. The text data were tokenized using SentencePiece (Kudo and Richardson, 2018) with the unigram setting (Kudo, 2018), trained on the training data with a 10k-token vocabulary size. The source audio was pre-processed with the SpecAugment data augmentation technique (Park et al., 2019), then the speech features (80 log Mel-filter banks) were extracted and Cepstral Mean and Variance Normalization was applied at global level. Samples with a length above 30s were filtered out. The configuration parameters are the default ones set by Ma et al. (2020).

Training settings Our SimulST systems are Transformer-based models (Vaswani et al., 2017), composed by 12 encoder layers, 6 decoder layers, 256 features for the attention layers and 2,048 hidden units in the feed-forward layers. All models are based on a custom version of Wang et al. (2020), having two initial 1D convolutional layers with *gelu* activation functions (Hendrycks and Gimpel, 2020), but adapted to the simultaneous scenario as per Ma et al. (2020). Moreover, the encoder self-attentions are biased using a logarithmic distance penalty (Di Gangi et al., 2019), leveraging the local context. Training was performed with cross entropy loss, Adam optimizer (Kingma and Ba, 2015) with a learning rate of 1e-4 with an inverse square-root scheduler and 4,000 warm-up updates. We set mini-batches of 5,000 max tokens and update the gradients every 16 mini-batches. The best checkpoint was selected based on the lowest cross entropy value on the MuST-Cinema dev set. READ/WRITE actions of the wait-k policy are decided by means of a pre-decision module at BPE (token) level (Ma et al., 2020). The adopted pre-decision module is fixed, which triggers the decision process at every pre-defined number of frames. Since a frame covers 10ms of the audio, an encoder state covers 40ms due to a 4x subsampling by the initial convolutional layers. Since the average length of a word in MuST-Cinema is 270ms, we consider 7 encoder states for a READ/WRITE action, which is the default parameter used by Ma et al. (2020), leading to a window size of 280ms. In order to explore the quality vs latency compromise and to study the effect of the system latency on the delay of the subtitles, we experimented with two values of k, resulting in wait-3 and wait-5 models. For comparison, we also trained one offline ST system per language.

Evaluation The evaluation focuses on two different aspects: 1) systems' performance and 2) display modes. For systems' performance, quality is evaluated with SacreBLEU (Post, 2018), which is computed on the ST output containing the subtitle breaks. The latency of the system is evaluated with Average Lagging (AL) (Ma et al., 2019) adapted to the ST scenario by Ma et al. (2020). In order to test the ability of the systems to generate properly formed subtitles, we evaluate the conformity to the length constraint (Len) as the percentage of subtitles having a length between 6 and 42 characters per line TED (2021). The display modes are evaluated in terms of reading speed and delay, as described in Section 3.3.

5 Results

5.1 Quality, Latency and Conformity

As far as quality is concerned (Table 1), the wait-3 strategy achieves low BLEU scores but there is significant improvement for wait-5, even reaching the performance of the offline system for French. These scores are in line with those reported in SimulST settings while in our setting the difficulty is exacerbated by the requirement to correctly place the subtitling breaks. In fact, the offline system, despite not being optimised for the offline mode, still performs comparatively or better than Karakanta et al. (2020a), who reported 18.76 BLEU points for French and 11.82 for German, while the length conformity is higher by 2%. As for latency (AL), we observe an increase between 0.2-0.6 seconds from wait-3 to wait-5, which lags behind by 2 seconds. Still, these spans are not higher than the Ear-to-Voice Span (EVS) threshold reported for intralingual respeaking (2.1 seconds) and way below the EVS for interlingual respeaking (4.1 secs) (Chmiel et al., 2017). This shows that, despite the poor quality, SimulST could have the potential of reducing the delay in interlingual live subtitling. In terms of proper subtitles, we found that our systems are capable of properly inserting the break symbols, despite the partial input they receive, since more than 90% of the generated subtitles conform to the length constraint. This ability of our SimulST systems is indispensable for taking advantage of the predicted structure of the subtitles to experiment with display modes in blocks and lines.

Model	**en-it**			**en-de**			**en-fr**		
	BLEU	AL	Len	BLEU	AL	Len	BLEU	AL	Len
offline	19.5	-	96%	14.0	-	96%	18.6	-	97%
wait-3	12.2	1755	91%	7.7	1422	94%	13.5	1570	92%
wait-5	15.1	1936	92%	11.1	2050	91%	18.1	2035	94%

Table 1: SacreBLEU (considering <eol> and <eob>), Average Lagging (AL) in ms and conformity to the length constraint (Len) on three language pairs of MuST-Cinema amara.

5.2 Display mode and reading speed

When comparing the reading speed (*rs*) of the three modes (Table 2), the word-for-word and block mode have the highest *rs* for the wait-5 and wait-3 strategy respectively. The standard deviation is much higher for the word-for-word mode, which indicates a large variation in the *rs*. This could be attributed to the SimulST systems' generation rate. The systems wait at the beginning of the utterance but, when the end of the input is reached, they perform greedy search and emit all remaining words at once. This rate leads to a jerky display of words, where some words remain on screen for a long time and others flush before the viewer manages to read them. However, the block mode has the lowest percentage of subtitles achieving a reading speed of max 21 cps. The problem of this mode is that each block remains on screen until the next <eob> is generated, which corresponds to the duration of the following block. For example, if a block of two lines with 40 characters each is followed by a block of one line of 25 characters, the first block would have a short time to be displayed, resulting in a high *rs*, and vice versa. One future direction would be to adjust the time of each block to better accommodate its reading speed, however, in initial experiments we found that this approach led to excessively high delay. Scrolling lines, our proposed method, achieves by far the lowest mean *rs*, with all models scoring below the 21 cps threshold. The same result is shown for the percentage of conforming subtitles, where conformity to reading speed reaches ~80%. It is worth noting that *rs* increases from wait-3 to wait-5 for the block and line modes for en→de, contrary to the other languages. This correlates with the lower percentage of length conformity (94% for wait-3 to 91% for wait-5) and shows the importance of correctly predicting the position of the breaks for the success of the display methods relying on these breaks.

As for delay, the word-for-word mode has the lowest delay, which corresponds to the system's lagging. The block mode has the highest delay, while our proposed method manages to reduce the delay by 0.6 seconds on average compared to the display in blocks, remaining close to a 4-second EVS. Our results are validated by the inversely proportional relationship between *rs* and delay. Scrolling lines, our proposed method, seems to achieve a fair compromise between a comfortable reading speed and an acceptable delay, while combining the benefits of the presence of the word on the right, less dynamic text and the preservation of the block structure which is familiar to most viewers.

	display mode	*wait-3*			*wait-5*		
		rs	$\leq$ 21 cps	delay	rs	$\leq$ 21 cps	delay
en-it	word	53.5 ± 9.9	61%	1755	40.1 ± 8.0	70%	1936
	block	53.4 ± 9.1	38%	4690	36.5 ± 7.0	62%	5004
	line	17.6 ± 5.2	79%	4092	14.4 ± 4.1	85%	4461
	display mode	*wait-3*			*wait-5*		
		rs	$\leq$ 21 cps	delay	rs	$\leq$ 21 cps	delay
en-de	word	29.1 ± 7.2	70%	1422	58.4 ± 10.5	63%	2050
	block	33.3 ± 6.2	37%	4772	52.6 ± 9.2	56%	4503
	line	12.4 ± 3.7	85%	4090	19.9 ± 5.4	78%	3894
	display mode	*wait-3*			*wait-5*		
		rs	$\leq$ 21 cps	delay	rs	$\leq$ 21 cps	delay
en-fr	word	39.7 ± 7.9	55%	1570	53.4 ± 9.0	57%	2035
	block	43.8 ± 7.6	37%	4872	46.1 ± 8.0	56%	5273
	line	15.4 ± 4.2	78%	4217	18.4 ± 4.8	78%	4708

Table 2: Reading speed (*rs*) mean and standard deviation in characters per second (cps), percentage of subtitles with a *rs* of max. 21 cps and display delay (in ms) on three language pairs of MuST-Cinema amara.

6 Conclusions

In this work we adapted SimulST systems for the task of live subtitling, by forcing the systems to generate subtitle breaks. We showed that SimulST systems are able to generate properly-formed subtitles. Given this finding, we moved on to explore display strategies alternative to the word-for-word display, the established display mode in SimulST. Word-for-word display is sub-optimal for readability and comprehension (Romero-Fresco, 2010). For automatically generated live subtitles, we found that it leads to an extremely variable reading speed, with some words lagging on the screen while the words towards the end of the utterance flushing through the screen. On the other hand, the display in blocks, which is the traditional mode for displaying offline subtitles, leads to a large delay and improves the reading speed only for SimulST systems with a higher latency. Our proposed display method, scrolling lines, is the only one achieving a comfortable mean reading speed below 21 cps, with around 80% of the subtitles having acceptable reading speed, while the delay remains along the 4-second threshold.

As for the feasibility of SimulST for live subtitling, there is still a long way to go in several directions. From a technical point of view, the principal issue is still the poor translation quality, which could benefit from advancements in tailored architectures. Evaluation marks progress in any field, but we still lack robust evaluation methodologies, taking into account all dimensions of the target medium, both quality and readability. Lastly, scholarly work is needed around user perception studies in automatic subtitling and live interlingual subtitling. Technology is moving faster than research and user studies are key to ensure our implementational efforts are moving in the right direction. We hope our work has set the ball rolling for further research in automatising live interlingual subtitling.

References

Alinejad, A., Siahbani, M., and Sarkar, A. (2018). Prediction improves simultaneous neural machine translation. In *Proceedings of the 2018 Conference on Empirical Methods in Natural Language Processing*, pages 3022–3027, Brussels, Belgium. Association for Computational Linguistics.

Arivazhagan, N., Cherry, C., Macherey, W., Chiu, C.-C., Yavuz, S., Pang, R., Li, W., and Raffel, C. (2019). Monotonic infinite lookback attention for simultaneous machine translation. In *Proceedings of the 57th Annual Meeting of the Association for Computational Linguistics*, pages 1313–1323, Florence, Italy. Association for Computational Linguistics.

Arivazhagan, N., Cherry, C., Macherey, W., and Foster, G. F. (2020). Re-translation versus streaming for simultaneous translation. In *IWSLT*.

Bojar, O., Macháček, D., Sagar, S., Smrž, O., Kratochvíl, J., Polák, P., Ansari, E., Mahmoudi, M., Kumar, R., Franceschini, D., Canton, C., Simonini, I., Nguyen, T.-S., Schneider, F., Stüker, S., Waibel, A., Haddow, B., Sennrich, R., and Williams, P. (2021). ELITR multilingual live subtitling: Demo and strategy. In *Proceedings of the 16th Conference of the European Chapter of the Association for Computational Linguistics: System Demonstrations*, pages 271–277, Online. Association for Computational Linguistics.

Bérard, A., Pietquin, O., Servan, C., and Besacier, L. (2016). Listen and Translate: A Proof of Concept for End-to-End Speech-to-Text Translation. In *NIPS Workshop on end-to-end learning for speech and audio processing*, Barcelona, Spain.

Chmiel, A., Szarkowska, A., Korzinek, D., Lijewska, A., Łukasz Dutka, Łukasz Brocki, and Marasek, K. (2017). Ear–voice span and pauses in intra- and interlingual respeaking: An exploratory study into temporal aspects of the respeaking process. *Applied Psycholinguistics*, 38:1201 – 1227.

Dawson, H. (2019). Feasibility, quality and assessment of interlingual live subtitling: A pilot study. *Journal of Audiovisual Translation*, 2(2):36–56.

Di Gangi, M. A., Negri, M., and Turchi, M. (2019). Adapting Transformer to End-to-End Spoken Language Translation. In *Proc. Interspeech 2019*, pages 1133–1137.

Elbayad, M., Besacier, L., and Verbeek, J. (2020). Efficient Wait-k Models for Simultaneous Machine Translation. In *Proc. Interspeech 2020*, pages 1461–1465.

Grissom II, A., He, H., Boyd-Graber, J., Morgan, J., and Daumé III, H. (2014). Don't until the final verb wait: Reinforcement learning for simultaneous machine translation. In *Proceedings of the 2014 Conference on Empirical Methods in Natural Language Processing (EMNLP)*, pages 1342–1352, Doha, Qatar. Association for Computational Linguistics.

Gu, J., Neubig, G., Cho, K., and Li, V. O. (2017). Learning to translate in real-time with neural machine translation. In *Proceedings of the 15th Conference of the European Chapter of the Association for Computational Linguistics: Volume 1, Long Papers*, pages 1053–1062, Valencia, Spain. Association for Computational Linguistics.

Hendrycks, D. and Gimpel, K. (2020). Gaussian Error Linear Units (GELUs).

Karakanta, A., Negri, M., and Turchi, M. (2020a). Is 42 the answer to everything in subtitling-oriented speech translation? In *Proceedings of the 17th International Conference on Spoken Language Translation*, pages 209–219, Online. Association for Computational Linguistics.

Karakanta, A., Negri, M., and Turchi, M. (2020b). MuST-cinema: a speech-to-subtitles corpus. In *Proceedings of the 12th Language Resources and Evaluation Conference*, pages 3727–3734, Marseille, France. European Language Resources Association.

Kingma, D. P. and Ba, J. (2015). Adam: A method for stochastic optimization. In Bengio, Y. and LeCun, Y., editors, *3rd International Conference on Learning Representations, ICLR 2015, San Diego, CA, USA, May 7-9, 2015, Conference Track Proceedings*.

Kudo, T. (2018). Subword Regularization: Improving Neural Network Translation Models with Multiple Subword Candidates. In *Proceedings of the 56th Annual Meeting of the Association for Computational Linguistics (Volume 1: Long Papers)*, pages 66–75, Melbourne, Australia. Association for Computational Linguistics.

Kudo, T. and Richardson, J. (2018). SentencePiece: A simple and language independent subword tokenizer and detokenizer for Neural Text Processing. In *Proceedings of the 2018 Conference on Empirical Methods in Natural Language Processing: System Demonstrations*, pages 66–71, Brussels, Belgium. Association for Computational Linguistics.

Lambourne, A. (2006). Subtitle respeaking. *Intralinea, Special Issue on Respeaking*.

Ma, M., Huang, L., Xiong, H., Zheng, R., Liu, K., Zheng, B., Zhang, C., He, Z., Liu, H., Li, X., Wu, H., and Wang, H. (2019). STACL: Simultaneous translation with implicit anticipation and controllable latency using prefix-to-prefix framework. In *Proceedings of the 57th Annual Meeting of the Association for Computational Linguistics*, pages 3025–3036, Florence, Italy. Association for Computational Linguistics.

Ma, X., Pino, J., and Koehn, P. (2020). SimulMT to SimulST: Adapting simultaneous text translation to end-to-end simultaneous speech translation. In *Proceedings of the 1st Conference of the Asia-Pacific Chapter of the Association for Computational Linguistics and the 10th International Joint Conference on Natural Language Processing*, pages 582–587, Suzhou, China. Association for Computational Linguistics.

Marsh, A. (2004). Simultaneous Interpreting and Respeaking: a Comparison. Master's thesis, University of Westminster, UK.

Netflix (2021). Timed text style guide: General requirements. https://partnerhelp.netflixstudios.com/hc/en-us/articles/215758617-Timed-Text-Style-Guide-General-Requirements. Last accessed: 10/06/2021.

Nguyen, H., Estève, Y., and Besacier, L. (2021). An empirical study of end-to-end simultaneous speech translation decoding strategies. In *ICASSP 2021-2021 IEEE International Conference on Acoustics, Speech and Signal Processing (ICASSP)*, pages 7528–7532. IEEE.

Ofcom (2005). Subtitling–an issue of speed? Technical report, Ofcom, London: Ofcom.

Ofcom (2015). Measuring live subtitling quality: Results from the fourth sampling exercise. Technical report, Ofcom, London: Office of Communications.

Park, D. S., Chan, W., Zhang, Y., Chiu, C.-C., Zoph, B., Cubuk, E. D., and Le, Q. V. (2019). SpecAugment: A Simple Data Augmentation Method for Automatic Speech Recognition. In *Proc. Interspeech 2019*, pages 2613–2617.

Perego, E., Missier, F. D., Porta, M., and Mosconi, M. (2010). The cognitive effectiveness of subtitle processing. *Media Psychology*, 13:243—272.

Post, M. (2018). A call for clarity in reporting BLEU scores. In *Proceedings of the Third Conference on Machine Translation: Research Papers*, pages 186–191, Brussels, Belgium. Association for Computational Linguistics.

Pöchhacker, F. and Remael, A. (2020). New efforts? a competence-oriented task analysis of interlingual live subtitling. *Linguistica Antverpiensia, New Series – Themes in Translation Studies*, 18(0).

Rajendran, D. J., Duchowski, A. T., Orero, P., Martínez, J., and Romero-Fresco, P. (2013). Effects of text chunking on subtitling: A quantitative and qualitative examination. *Perspectives*, 21(1):5–21.

Rayner, K., Liversedge, S. P., and White, S. J. (2006). Eye movements when reading disappearing text: The importance of the word to the right of fixation. *Vision Research*, pages 310—323.

Ren, Y., Liu, J., Tan, X., Zhang, C., Qin, T., Zhao, Z., and Liu, T.-Y. (2020). SimulSpeech: End-to-end simultaneous speech to text translation. In *Proceedings of the 58th Annual Meeting of the Association for Computational Linguistics*, pages 3787–3796, Online. Association for Computational Linguistics.

Romero-Fresco, P. (2010). *Standing on quicksand: hearing viewers' comprehension and reading patterns of respoken subtitles for the news*, pages 175 – 194. Brill, Leiden, The Netherlands.

Romero-Fresco, P. (2011). *Subtitling through speech recognition: Respeaking*. Manchester: St. Jerome.

Romero-Fresco, P. (2015). Final thoughts: Viewing speed in subtitling. *The Reception of Subtitles for the Deaf and Hard of Hearing in Europe*, pages 335–341.

Sharmin, S., Wiklund, S. M.-A., and Tiittula, L. (2016). The reading process of dynamic text – a linguistic approach to an eye movement study. *SKY Journal of Linguistics*, pages 119–146.

Szarkowska, A. (2016). Report on the results of an online survey on subtitle presentation times and line breaks in interlingual subtitling. part 1: Subtitlers. Technical report, London: University College London.

TED (2021). Subtitling tips. https://www.ted.com/participate/translate/subtitling-tips.

Vaswani, A., Shazeer, N., Parmar, N., Uszkoreit, J., Jones, L., Gomez, A. N., Kaiser, L. u., and Polosukhin, I. (2017). Attention is all you need. In Guyon, I., Luxburg, U. V., Bengio, S., Wallach, H., Fergus, R., Vishwanathan, S., and Garnett, R., editors, *Advances in Neural Information Processing Systems*, volume 30. Curran Associates, Inc.

Wang, C., Tang, Y., Ma, X., Wu, A., Okhonko, D., and Pino, J. (2020). fairseq s2t: Fast speech-to-text modeling with fairseq. In *Proceedings of the 2020 Conference of the Asian Chapter of the Association for Computational Linguistics (AACL): System Demonstrations*.

Weiss, R. J., Chorowski, J., Jaitly, N., Wu, Y., and Chen, Z. (2017). Sequence-to-Sequence Models Can Directly Translate Foreign Speech. In *Proceedings of Interspeech 2017*, pages 2625–2629, Stockholm, Sweden.

Zheng, B., Liu, K., Zheng, R., Ma, M., Liu, H., and Huang, L. (2020). Simultaneous translation policies: From fixed to adaptive. *ArXiv*, abs/2004.13169.

Zheng, B., Zheng, R., Ma, M., and Huang, L. (2019a). Simpler and faster learning of adaptive policies for simultaneous translation. In *Proceedings of the 2019 Conference on Empirical Methods in Natural Language Processing and the 9th International Joint Conference on Natural Language Processing (EMNLP-IJCNLP)*, pages 1349–1354, Hong Kong, China. Association for Computational Linguistics.

Zheng, B., Zheng, R., Ma, M., and Huang, L. (2019b). Simultaneous translation with flexible policy via restricted imitation learning. In *Proceedings of the 57th Annual Meeting of the Association for Computational Linguistics*, pages 5816–5822, Florence, Italy. Association for Computational Linguistics.

Technology-Augmented Multilingual Communication Models: New Interaction Paradigms, Shifts in the Language Services Industry, and Implications for Training Programs

Francesco Saina f.saina@ssmlcarlobo.it
SSML Carlo Bo, Rome and Bari, Italy

Abstract

This paper explores how technology, particularly digital tools and artificial intelligence, are impacting multilingual communication and language transfer processes. Information and communication technologies are enabling novel interaction patterns, with computers transitioning from pure media to actual language generators, and profoundly reshaping the industry of language services, as the relevance of language data and assisting engines continues to rise. Since these changes deeply affect communication and languages models overall, they need to be addressed not only from the perspective of information technology or by business-driven companies, but also in the field of translation and interpreting studies, in a broader debate among scholars and practitioners, and when preparing educational programs for the training of specialised language professionals. Special focus is devoted to some of the latest advancements in automatic speech recognition and spoken translation, and how their applications in interpreting may push the boundaries of new 'augmented' real-world use cases. Hence, this work—at the intersection of theoretical investigation, professional practice, and instructional design—aims at offering an introductory overview of the current landscape and envisaging potential paths for forthcoming scenarios.

1 Language Technologies

Information and digital technologies have had a profound impact on society and communication over the past decades and even more in the last few years. Statistical and neural systems are at the foundation of many high-tech and 'intelligent' solutions employed in almost any domain nowadays, including language—in all its dimensions and areas of application.

Computers and devices process and analyse language data for several purposes (from text analysis and speech recognition to data mining and information retrieval) by applying the models of computational linguistics and natural language processing (NLP).

Today, applications of language technologies include automatic speech recognition (ASR) systems providing dictation and transcription, voice assistants, chatbots, spelling and grammar checkers, writing assistants, speech synthesis, and interactive voice response (IVR) systems, just to name a few.

However, research in the field is seldom public or shared since it often deals with trade secrets of the companies that hold such valuable technology and know-how, which they also leverage for the related remarkable commercial value. Moreover, as it will be recalled later, publications on the topic are often confined to computer science (CS)—despite language technologies entailing a multi- and interdisciplinary approach by their very nature.

1.1 Translation Technologies

In the space of language transfer processes, traditionally associated with the spheres of translation and interpreting, technology has also gradually achieved a prominent position.

Language databases such as translation memories (TMs) and termbases are largely used and leveraged by translators not only to improve their speed and productivity, but also their consistency and accuracy. These resources are integrated in software platforms referred to as translation environment tools (TEnTs) and are already regularly introduced to students of university programs in translation.

Over the years, the use of computer-assisted translation (CAT) tools has also gradually incorporated automated or machine translation (MT) engines, which not only aid human translators in their task, but are also capable of offering interlingual rendering as a standalone solution.

In the digital space, billions of words needing scalable and immediate interlingual adaptation are produced every day, and human translators simply cannot keep pace with these volumes. Therefore, first and foremost, MT is (and cannot avoid being) used in the localization processes of this content, and the significant enhancement of output quality derived from the disruptive introduction of neural machine translation (NMT) helped reducing the gap between human-crafted and machine-generated translation quality.

Nonetheless, performance and output levels are still not consistent across all language pairs and domains, due to varying volumes and quality of relevant training data—currently, the main areas of research interest in this field include precisely the study of models and systems to meet the challenge of the so-called low-resource languages (the majority of human languages, still lacking sufficient monolingual or parallel corpora or manually-crafted resources to build functional statistical NLP applications) (Magueresse et al., 2020; Conia and Navigli, 2020).

Following the large-scale use of MT and translation technologies in the real world and their integration in the localization workflows of language service providers, they also gradually made their way into training programs for translators, with at least some modules dedicated to them (Pym, 2013; Sikora and Walczyński, 2015).

1.2 Interpreting Technologies

Conversely, in the area of spoken translation, i.e. interpreting, the adoption and integration of technology-based systems in the workflows and practice of interpreters has been slower and less far-reaching (Fantinuoli, 2018).

Tools aiding practitioners in some of their activities (from the preparation phase to actual 'in-booth' support, e.g. glossary creation and management, terminology extraction and research), fall under the category of computer-assisted interpreting (CAI).

Partially because of its limited representation in interpreting literature, the 'technological shift' in the profession is still underway, although developments and interest in interpreting technologies are considerably growing (Prandi, 2017)—also due to the latest breakthroughs in remote or distance interpreting, while other applications remain still largely unexplored.

Indeed, only recently, following a steadily growing production of multimedia content, machine interpreting (also referred to as automatic spoken translation or speech translation) has gained momentum both in academic and commercial environments, especially in the perspective of transitioning from current cascade to more promising end-to-end models.

The single modules comprising the concatenated cascade approach (automatic speech recognition or speech-to-text, machine translation, and speech synthesis or text-to-speech) have significantly improved thanks to the high volumes and quality of task-targeted training data, and consequently this remains the most frequently adopted approach to date.

1.3 A Vision for Language AI

Nevertheless, observation, analysis, and evaluation of all the applications of language technologies mentioned above are largely conducted in the framework of information technology (IT) and CS.

Besides a valuable branch of research on translator–computer interaction (O'Brien, 2012; Ferreira and Schwieter, 2017) and translation process research (TRP) (Ferreira and Schwieter, 2015; Carl et al., 2016; Jakobsen, 2017), no systematic investigation experiences and patterns seem to have developed from the broader perspective and in the fields of communication, language, and translation and interpreting (T&I) studies.

However, multilingual activities, translation, and interpreting are first and foremost communication events—not only mere information or transposition processes.

Hence the need to promote a different approach and embrace a novel vision in academic and professional communities of language practitioners to create a wider theoretical and attitudinal framework.

T&I studies and CS ought to increasingly inform each other to mutually improve efficiency, optimise processes and workflows, and even imagine and design new scenarios for the introduction of language applications in technology-enabled use cases.

Hesitancy (or even reluctance) towards technology among a segment of language practitioners seems to be due to a lack of trust in the tools, considering them as a source of distraction and additional cognitive load, or scarcely effective and satisfactory (Tripepi Winteringham, 2010; Corpas Pastor and Fern, 2016; Fantinuoli, 2019), but also partly as a result of an approach to artificial intelligence (AI) as opposed to human intelligence or humans outright.

Beyond the possible semantic reasons behind that (the word 'artificial' may be associated with something unnatural, insincere, or fraudulent), the whole narration around AI should be reconsidered to facilitate its acceptance and enjoyment.

Some of the most evident benefits brought to language services by this technological revolution (speed, productivity, accuracy, consistency) suggest that the main advantages derive from automation (Herrmann, 2018). Automated processes can undoubtedly be seen as a winning facet, since they reduce and optimise repetitive and unproductive steps of processes, and ensure more time and resources are devoted to highly demanding tasks. Automated intelligence (and intelligent—or smart—automation) can definitely be introduced to all current and aspiring practitioners, as well as end users and customers, since they do not represent a risk for the parties involved.

As a consequence, by accomplishing such delegated tasks, AI can enhance human activity without replacing human decisions and responsibility, yet supporting and augmenting the possibilities and outreach of human performance. In this respect, along with the above-mentioned 'automated intelligence', an additional facet of AI to be endorsed would also be that of 'augmented intelligence' (Floridi et al., 2018).

Indeed, translation and interpreting professional communities are already starting to refer to technology-supported language transfer processes as augmented translation and interpreting, and the next shift could be from computer-assisted to computer-augmented language services (DePalma, 2017).

Finally, the scientific community is also progressively starting to suggest a different meaning for the second term of this phraseme, acknowledging that in modern digital tools 'intelligence' does not coincide with human-like 'cleverness', but rather with 'smartness' and 'agency', i.e. the ability to successfully solve problems or complete specific tasks (Kelly, 2017; Floridi, 2019; Crawford, 2021)—thus confirming the overall perspective described in the above paragraphs.

2 Combining Language and Computer Studies

2.1 New Interaction Paradigms

Media and artefacts have a deep impact on the message they carry and directly shape the structure and nature of communication itself (McLuhan, 1964), affecting the way the message is perceived, and consequently how both senders and receivers think and behave.

Early on in their history, it became clear that computers were going to enable and facilitate communication among humans, rather than directly interact with them (Licklider and Taylor, 1968). For decades, machines have subsequently been a medium for human interaction, with varying preeminence attributed to written and spoken language.

Language has always been the distinctive feature characterizing humanity and differentiating it from any other intelligent species or living being. In particular, speaking has traditionally been the natural channel for spontaneous interaction, while writing has primarily been used for information storage or formal communication, but these roles have alternated repeatedly (even only over the last century) following a sequence of favoured communication channels (printing, telephone and mass media, internet and instant messaging tools) throughout history.

However, with the recent development of neural networks and deep learning algorithms, information and communication technologies (ICTs) are starting to act not only as pure intermediaries (as communication artefacts have always been), but—to a certain extent—also as 'autonomous' and original language and content generators.

Presumably, technology (not only language technology) will increasingly integrate with human senses by moving from external hardware to wearable devices, ultimately changing everyday communication paradigms and human interaction with reality (Sayers et al., 2021).

Despite being still distant from complete satisfactory performance (since they largely depend on training data and would require a higher degree of 'intelligence' to advance), generative language models are a reality with real-world applications in a few niche industries already.

This area is still in its infancy, yet its groundbreaking role and societal impact cannot be ignored. If hereinbefore only humans had enjoyed the privilege of holding the exclusive property of language, now a new active player is entering the scene, i.e. machines and technological artefacts (Benanti, 2021). This will have serious and unavoidable implications on communication patterns (Floridi and Chiriatti, 2020) which are still to be adequately explored.

2.2 Shifts in Multilingual Communication and the Language Services Industry

The study and assessment of language technologies in CS is commonly product-oriented and primarily takes into consideration parameters such as output quality (as compared to benchmark reference translations or datasets), usability, or technical performance.

Conversely, T&I studies—besides the long-standing debate on the definition of quality and evaluation methodologies (House, 2015; Moorkens et al., 2018; Chatzikoumi, 2020; Rivera-Trigueros, 2021)—generally consider criteria including functional equivalence, faithfulness, intelligibility, and the facilitation of communicative interaction (Pöchhacker, 2001).

Only recently, have scholars in the field of T&I studies started observing language technologies from a more comprehensive language and communication viewpoint, thus hopefully paving the way to a new area of research and study combining T&I and CS.

The intersection of the two disciplines could benefit both language and technology experts—the former, typically lacking deep practical technical knowledge to design and develop digital tools and resources to support them, could leverage technological insights to their advantage, whereas the latter would better understand the potential linguistic, communicative, and societal consequences of current and emerging technologies.

Especially in the field of real-time multilingual communication, besides simultaneous interpretation—still the most resorted-to activity for this task—this field could soon include other modalities such as interlingual respeaking, automated speech-to-text translation, live subtitling, and instant multilingual information retrieval or key concepts extraction.

The results of early testing (Fantinuoli and Prandi, 2021) show a better performance by humans in terms of intelligibility (i.e. the perception of the target text in terms of fluency, clarity, and adequacy) and a more accurate performance by machines in terms of informativeness (i.e. the evaluation of the target text in terms of content and semantic information in comparison with the source text).

Considering that automated speech translation systems do not provide completely satisfactory outcomes by themselves yet, the current focus of research should be on how digital systems can integrate human work, by supporting and enhancing human-performed activities (Desmet et al., 2018). This is what is happening in most other professions (where technology integrates and improves the effectiveness of several tasks), including written translation, as the use of CAT tools and resources like TMs, termbases, and MT is already part of almost any translator's toolkit.

In addition to the implementations described in section 1, AI and machine learning (ML) are also propelling translation and localization processes by automating workflows to meet tighter turnaround times and incorporating computer-generated translation as a final product or as the basis for activities like machine translation post-editing (MTPE) and machine-assisted subtitling (MAS)—even in fields where it seemed inconceivable until not long ago, such as medicine and life sciences or the media and entertainment industry.

In this direction, innovation departments of companies, academic research projects, and even institutions and international organizations have begun to explore the usability of newer-generation and AI-empowered CAI tools too, where ASR provides in-session support to human interpreters in relation to problem triggers such as numbers, unit conversions, acronyms, named entities, and specialised terminology (Defrancq and Fantinuoli, 2021).

At the same time, both language service providers (often also referred to as translation agencies) and individual practitioners are diversifying and redirecting their offer from strictly language-related activities to broader adjacent AI-related language needs, including training data creation, collection, annotation, and validation.

3 Renovating Language Programs and Vocational Training

Just like research on language technologies (and technology for language practitioners) needs to overcome the boundaries of CS to enter T&I studies too, the time has also come for training programs—both university degrees for aspiring linguists as well as vocational training and continuing professional development (CPD) courses—to systematically integrate all of this in the classrooms.

To achieve the desired outcome, a holistic and integrated implementation approach is required. Indeed, current challenges in the realization of such programs include—but are not limited to—the diverse backgrounds and expertise degrees of both trainees and trainers (since they are still typically formally trained in either one of the two environments) and the compelling necessity to design curricula in which technology is not a mere supplement segregated to specific courses, but rather an element underlying the structure of programs and a tool regularly available to trainees.

3.1 The Need for Consistent Training in Language Technologies

First, this is because research in the field and on the actual products should not be an exclusive domain of private corporations (often the so-called 'big-tech' companies or businesses receiving massive funding), but also stem from the academia and institutional centres. Given their potential communicative and societal impact, these tools should not be developed in search of improving performance and economic profit only, and the related information is worth being widely accessible.

At the same time, CS—and especially AI, since it inherently entails (or at least aims at establishing) an interaction with basically any aspect of the real world—are required to welcome contributions from other disciplines. Interdisciplinarity can be more broadly (and metaphorically) conceived as the creation of 'neural networks' of studies by assimilating epistemological concepts along with analytical and research practices form other specialties.

Finally, and most importantly, the labour market is increasingly requiring the new generations of language professionals to be experts who can combine their domain expertise and knowledge with digital and IT skills (Sikora, 2014). As some institutions* across the world have already started doing (Diño, 2021), and in response to the needs for new industry roles, language and T&I programs are to include language programming modules—and most linguists are to add coding to their arsenal—since language services and language technologies will only be increasingly intertwined. Translators and interpreters will probably be no longer allowed to disregard NLP and computational linguistics, and language engineers will inevitably work closer to language service providers.

A widespread concern among human language professionals is to be eventually replaced by machines in their job. Indeed, a substantial share of the lower-end translation demand is already met by MT, with translators intervening in emerging human- or expert-in-the-loop models by fine-tuning the work of engines, or addressing highly specialised niches otherwise.

The same could happen with speech translation, with some portions of the labour space being taken over by automated spoken translation systems, when communication is particularly linear and unstratified. Similarly to what is already happening with written translation, humans would therefore progressively be covering high-end needs, where more than a plain linguistic equivalence is necessary, e.g. when managing different legal systems or requiring compliance with diverse regulations.

As a consequence, with greater availability of good-quality automated translations, expectations towards human language professionals are going to be even higher. This will be an additional challenge for practitioners and training institutions alike, being demanded a broader yet solid preparation as well as narrowing subject matter expertise.

Heading towards that direction, language professionals will be expected to offer trustworthiness—both for validating and enhancing machine work as well as performing the activity firsthand—rather than simple language support (Pym, 2020).

Technology and AI have gained a pivotal role in almost any professional activity, and NLP resources prove useful and effective in many instances of reality (Tavosanis, 2018), therefore successful human–machine synergy can only revamp the offer of language transfer solutions, and advance the accuracy and efficiency of practitioners to help them excel.

---

*For instance, the consortium of universities promoting the pioneering European Master's in Technology for Translation and Interpreting (EM TTI) offers a program combining computational linguistics and NLP with translation and interpreting technologies: https://em-tti.eu/.

3.2 Research and Training in Translation and Interpreting Technologies

However, as previously outlined, a remarkable share of translators and even more interpreters are still not familiar with IT resources already at their fingertips. Therefore, in addition to programming languages, another gap in skills and mindset needs to be bridged.

In training environments, research and professional practice should increasingly nurture one other by designing didactic methodologies and tools that would blend vocational and academic elements, and instruct qualified professionals who are in step with the times (Orlando, 2016).

Curricula should already devote at least some modules providing a framework for learning translation and interpreting technologies to gradually increase the awareness and proficiency of students with such systems (Fantinuoli and Prandi, 2018).

Nevertheless, courses cannot only aim at teaching the basics of the tools in an effort to chase resources which are already established in the 'real world', but institutions should notably be the driving space where those innovations are primarily experimented or even envisaged or designed.

For instance, post-editing and remote interpreting should not only be taught to translation and interpreting trainees once they become established practice on the professional market, but they should—and could—have been introduced when they were still expected to be 'the next big things' in the related fields.

Likewise, T&I programs should now consistently design courses enabling trainees to familiarise with the resources and frameworks they are likely to encounter in the early stages of their careers (namely in a very near future), i.e. language coding and programming, language data management, automated and machine-assisted translation and localization workflows, and CAI tools, just to name a few.

Once again, alongside practical abilities and know-how, an open and longsighted attitude would be the key for aspiring and established practitioners alike to embrace and even lead future advancement. Trainees should not only be learning how IT tools actually work, but also how to conceive and approach them in a process of true technological literacy (Kornacki, 2018), with valuable integrations from disciplines such as human–computer interaction and interaction design.

4 Future Scenarios and Final Remarks

The foundation for the introductory overview outlined in this work is considering language transfer processes as communication acts, rather than mere information or lexical correspondence. This is the reason for encouraging the inclusion of language technology studies within a wider communicative framework.

Text-based language technologies already significantly impacted human communication and human–machine interaction patterns, and written translation activities are extensively benefitting from numerous applications.

These innovations have already had a critical impact on how communication is performed with regards to language solutions. For instance, search engine optimization (SEO) has overturned how online content is conceived and put into words. Machine translation (MT) too has influenced the way global content and texts addressed to international audiences are drafted, to such an extent that pre-editing has become common practice for globalization service providers. Likewise, the long-term influence MT has even on the language used by translators and post-editors is worth further investigation.

On the other hand, fast-paced improvements are also shedding a new light on voice-based language technologies, whose consideration is turning from accessibility to full productivity resources with other paradigm shifts on the horizon.

Just like language varies diaphasically depending on context, e.g. with 'baby talk' and 'foreigner talk', the same may presumably happen when communicating to computers by resorting to specific 'computer-' or 'machine talk'.

Since these technologies amplify diamesic variations in the use of language, it can be reasonably expected that speech addressed to machines will become different from spontaneous verbal expression. That could only be consolidated over time by society becoming accustomed to interacting with machines through voice, as well as an increasingly blurred dividing line between spoken and written language (due to the ubiquitous usage of mobile devices, chats, and voice messages) and a machine-induced alignment to common cognitive structures representing the linguistic knowledge of speakers of any language (Chomsky, 1957, 1965).

Furthermore, text-based NLP applications like pre-filled responses or suggested writing hint at how much human communication relies upon automatic and perfunctory mechanisms, and how many interactions can truly be managed with little 'intelligence' or language understanding.

Still, it seems unlikely that communicators will completely adapt their speaking style to the outreach (and limits) of digital tools in some sort of pre-editing process of their talks. As conference speakers never adapted their rhetoric to the modality they were being interpreted with (e.g. simultaneous or consecutive), it will not happen with machine talk or computer-assisted interpreting either. Nonetheless, it is also true that real-world environments are becoming increasingly 'AI-friendly', i.e. ever more shaped around the abilities of computational artefacts (Floridi, 2019).

At first, it is far more likely—as practice with support tools already proves to practitioners who make use of them—that interpreters may alter and adjust their interpreting techniques to the performance and output of these resources and their prompts. Albeit machine talk still looks distant from real-world use cases, computer(-assisted) interpreting talk could more reasonably be an emerging trend.

After all, all communicative acts—just like all translations—are built around degrees of negotiation (Eco, 2003), in which communication is adjusted according to the behaviour of interlocutors, their use of language, their relationship, context, and levels of compromise.

Research in common sense AI is also trying to narrow the gap with in-context human language models (e.g. when deixis is in place) by studying new training methods that would enable technology to detect and exploit elements from the multimodal real world. 'Vokenization', as a combination of visual and language training datasets, is one of the most interesting examples of this (Tan and Bansal, 2020). Visual-language models may produce astounding enhancements in robotic assistants or automated subtitling and dubbing, where both verbal and non-verbal traits play equivalent roles.

Despite the existing limits of language technologies and still high word error rate (WER) scores in the performance of ASR dampen the enthusiasm towards silver bullet AI solutions, there are numerous operating resources not even specifically designed for translators or interpreters (like multilingual semantic networks and knowledge graphs, or named entity recognition and terminology extraction tools) which can turn out to be valuable assets (Rodríguez et al., 2021).

As linguists become acquainted with technological tools, proficiently learn to use them, and consequently improve their performance, further experimental assessments even on a remodelled and tailored version of Turing's (1950) popular testing for computer intelligence could be investigated to detect and observe the difference in outputs from language practitioners who make use of IT support tools and those who do not.

Ultimately, technology should not be conceived as an impending threat aiming at replacing humans, but as a resource providing support to ingeniously achieve the best possible cooperation between human abilities and computational efficiency.

This objective can be attained by thoroughly considering springing communication paradigms to bolster high-quality training data and valuable language resources (ELRC, 2019) and, above all, by adequately educating practitioners for a critical, accountable, and transparent use of language technology.

References

Benanti, P. (2021). *La grande invenzione: Il linguaggio come tecnologia dalle pitture rupestri al GPT-3*. San Paolo, Cinisello Balsamo (Milan).

Carl, M., et al. (eds.) (2016). *New Directions in Empirical Translation Process Research*. Springer, Cham.

Chatzikoumi, E. (2020). How to evaluate machine translation: A review of automated and human metrics. *Natural Language Engineering*, 26(2):137–161. https://doi.org/10.1017/S1351324919000469.

Chomsky, N. (1957). *Syntactic Structures*. Mouton, The Hague.

Chomsky, N. (1965). *Aspects of the Theory of Syntax*. MIT Press, Cambridge.

Conia, S., and Navigli, R. (2020). Conception: Multilingually-Enhanced, Human-Readable Concept Vector Representations. In *Proceedings of the 28th International Conference on Computational Linguistics*, pages 3268–3284, International Committee on Computational Linguistics, Barcelona. http://dx.doi.org/10.18653/v1/2020.coling-main.291.

Corpas Pastor, G., and Fern, L.M. (2016). *A Survey of Interpreters' Needs and Practices Related to Language Technology*. Universidad de Málaga, Málaga.

Crawford, K. (2021). *Atlas of AI: Power, Politics, and the Planetary Costs of Artificial Intelligence*. Yale University Press, New Haven.

Defrancq, B., and Fantinuoli, C. (2021). Automatic speech recognition in the booth: Assessment of system performance, interpreters' performances and interactions in the context of numbers. *Target*, 33(1):73–102. https://doi.org/10.1075/target.19166.def.

DePalma, D.A. (2017). Augmented Translation Powers up Language Services. *CSA Research*. https://csa-research.com/Blogs-Events/Blog/ArticleID/140.

Desmet, B., et al. (2018). Simultaneous interpretation of numbers and the impact of technological support. In Fantinuoli, C. (ed.). *Interpreting and technology*: 13–27. Language Science Press, Berlin.

Diño, G. (2021). Translators, Meet Python: Most Popular Programming Language for Student Linguists. *Slator*. https://slator.com/academia/translators-meet-python-most-popular-programming-language-for-student-linguists/.

Eco, U. (2003). *Mouse or Rat?: Translation as Negotiation*. Weidenfeld & Nicolson, London.

European Language Resource Coordination (ELRC) (2019). *ELRC White Paper*. ELRC Consortium, Saarbrücken. https://www.lr-coordination.eu/sites/default/files/Documents/ELRCWhitePaper.pdf.

Fantinuoli, C. (ed.) (2018). *Interpreting and technology*. Language Science Press, Berlin.

Fantinuoli, C., and Prandi, B. (2018). Teaching information and communication technologies: A proposal for the interpreting classroom. *trans-kom*, 11(2):162–182. http://www.trans-kom.eu/bd11nr02/trans-kom_11_02_02_Fantinouli_Prandi_Teaching.20181220.pdf.

Fantinuoli, C. (2019). The Technological Turn in Interpreting: The Challenges That Lie Ahead. In *Proceedings of the BDÜ Conference Translating and Interpreting 4.0*, pages 334–354, Bern.

Fantinuoli, C., and Prandi, B. (2021). *Towards the evaluation of simultaneous speech translation from a communicative perspective*. https://arxiv.org/pdf/2103.08364.pdf.

Ferreira, A., and Schwieter, J.W. (eds.) (2015). *Psycholinguistic and Cognitive Inquiries into Translation and Interpreting*. John Benjamins Publishing Company, Amsterdam.

Ferreira, A., and Schwieter, J.W. (eds.) (2017). *The Handbook of Translation and Cognition*. Wiley Blackwell, Hoboken.

Floridi, L., et al. (2018). AI4People—An Ethical Framework for a Good AI Society: Opportunities, Risks, Principles, and Recommendations. *Minds & Machines*, 28:689–707. https://doi.org/10.1007/s11023-018-9482-5.

Floridi, L. (2019). What the Near Future of Artificial Intelligence Could Be. *Philosophy & Technology*, 32:1–15. https://doi.org/10.1007/s13347-019-00345-y.

Floridi, L., and Chiriatti, M. (2020). GPT-3: Its Nature, Scope, Limits, and Consequences. *Minds & Machines*, 30:681–694. https://doi.org/10.1007/s11023-020-09548-1.

Herrmann, B. (2018). Global Content Needs Automated Intelligence as Much as Intelligent Automation. *EContent Magazine*. http://www.econtentmag.com/Articles/Editorial/Commentary/Global-Content-Needs-Automated-Intelligence-as-Much-as-Intelligent-Automation-124415.htm.

House, J. (2015). *Translation Quality Assessment: Past and Present*. Routledge, London.

Jakobsen, A.L. (2017). Translation Process Research. In Ferreira, A., and Schwieter, J.W. (eds.). *The Handbook of Translation and Cognition*: 21–49. Wiley Blackwell, Hoboken.

Kelly, K. (2017). *The Inevitable: Understanding the 12 Technological Forces That Will Shape Our Future*. Penguin, New York.

Kornacki, M. (2018). *Computer-Assisted Translation (CAT) Tools in the Translator Training Process*. Peter Lang, Bern.

Licklider, J.C.R., and Taylor, R.W. (1968). The Computer as a Communication Device. *Science and Technology*, 76(2):21–31.

Magueresse, A., et al. (2020). *Low-resource Languages: A Review of Past Work and Future Challenges*. https://arxiv.org/pdf/2006.07264v1.pdf.

McLuhan, M. (1964). *Understanding Media: The Extensions of Man*. McGraw-Hill, New York.

Moorkens, J., et al. (eds.) (2018). *Translation Quality Assessment: From Principles to Practice*. Springer, Cham.

O'Brien, S. (2012). Translation as Human–Computer Interaction. *Translation Spaces*, 1:101–122. https://doi.org/10.1075/ts.1.05obr.

Orlando, M. (2016). *Training 21st century translators and interpreters: At the crossroads of practice, research and pedagogy*. Frank & Timme GmbH.

Pöchhacker, F. (2001). Quality Assessment in Conference and Community Interpreting. *Meta*, 46(2):410–425. https://doi.org/10.7202/003847ar.

Prandi, B. (2017). Designing a Multimethod Study on the Use of CAI Tools during Simultaneous Interpreting. In *Proceedings of the 39th Conference Translating and the Computer*, pages 76–88, London.

Pym, A. (2013). Translation Skill-Sets in a Machine-Translation Age. *Meta*, 58(3):487–503. https://doi.org/10.7202/1025047ar.

Pym, A. (2020). The translation market, technology, and selling trustworthiness. Talk at the *7th National Symposium on Business English Linguistics*, Beijing Language and Culture University. https://youtu.be/TsEbU83cd_c.

Rivera-Trigueros, I. (2021). Machine translation systems and quality assessment: a systematic review. *Language Resources and Evaluation*. https://doi.org/10.1007/s10579-021-09537-5.

Rodríguez, S., et al. (2021). SmarTerp: A CAI System to Support Simultaneous Interpreters in Real-Time. In *Proceedings of the Translation and Interpreting Technology Online (TRITON) 2021 Conference*, pages 86–93. https://doi.org/10.26615/978-954-452-071-7_010.

Sayers, D., et al. (2021). *The Dawn of the Human-Machine Era: A forecast of new and emerging language technologies*. Report for EU COST Action CA19102 'Language In The Human-Machine Era' (LITHME). https://doi.org/10.17011/jyx/reports/20210518/1.

Sikora, I. (2014). The Need for CAT Training within Translator Training Programmes: Modern Bare Necessities or Unnecessary Fancies of Translation Trainers?. *inTRAlinea* (Special Issue: Challenges in Translation Pedagogy). http://www.intralinea.org/specials/article/2092.

Sikora, I., and Walczyński, M. (2015). Incorporating CAT tools and ICT in the translation and interpreting training at the undergraduate level. In Grabowski, Ł., and Piotrowski, T. (eds.). *The Translator and the Computer 2*: 119–133. Philological School of Higher Education, Wrocław.

Tan, H., and Bansal, M. (2020). *Vokenization: Improving Language Understanding with Contextualized, Visual-Grounded Supervision*. https://arxiv.org/abs/2010.06775.

Tavosanis, M. (2018). *Lingue e intelligenza artificiale*. Carocci, Roma.

Tripepi Winteringham, S. (2010). The usefulness of ICTs in interpreting practice. *The Interpreters' Newsletter*, 15:87–99.

Turing, A.M. (1950). Computing Machinery and Intelligence. *Mind*, LIX(236):433–446.

Association for Computational Linguistics
209 N. Eighth Street
Stroudsburg, Pennsylvania 18360

ISBN 978-1-7138-3923-1